By permission of The Perry Pictures Company, Malden, Massachusetts

Commonwealth of Massachusetts

Department of Education

1937, Number 5   Whole Number, 306

HORACE MANN
CENTENNIAL
1837   1937

Suggestions for Suitable Commemoration by the
Schools of Massachusetts of the One Hundredth
Anniversary of the Establishment of the Board
of Education in Massachusetts, and the Election
of Horace Mann as its First Secretary.

Issued by
Massachusetts Department of Education
JAMES G. REARDON, *Commissioner*

40M—7-'37, No. 1189

Printed by the Walter A. Smith Company,
Boston, Massachusetts.

CONTENTS

ILLUSTRATIONS

END PIECES

The illustrations in the text are the work of Miss Elizabeth H. Balcom of the Massachusetts School of Art. The cover design and the border around the Sonnet are the work of Miss Elvira Culotta, also of the Massachusetts School of Art.

HORACE MANN

Out of the "Old Bay State," a dreamer came.
All flesh goes down to dust, but vision stays
To serve mankind; in memory, we praise
The monumental work that brought him fame.
The steady purpose of his plan to share
With men of commonplace an enriched mind,
Will place him with all other great, who find
Their souls at peace in God's Eternal care.

Now tho he rests in gray cold cell of stone,
His name, like luminaries held in air,
Emblazons through posterity his dare
That all should sip of wisdom, none alone.
His deeds are registered where records are
Illuminated by a chartered star.

— BLANCHE D. SAMPSON,
Holyoke, Mass.

CHAPTER 4

RESOLVE PROVIDING FOR A PROCLAMATION BY THE GOVERNOR
RELATIVE TO OBSERVANCES DURING THE CURRENT YEAR IN
COMMEMORATION OF THE DISTINGUISHED PUBLIC SERVICE OF
HORACE MANN.

Whereas, Horace Mann served with marked distinction as a member of the General Court during the years eighteen hundred and twenty-seven to eighteen hundred and thirty-seven and was the president of the senate in the years eighteen hundred and thirty-six and eighteen hundred and thirty-seven; and

Whereas, In the year eighteen hundred and thirty-seven he accepted the secretaryship of the board of education of this commonwealth, which board was established in said year; and

Whereas, His labor in behalf of free education and improved standards of instruction have immortalized his name; and

Whereas, The year nineteen hundred and thirty-seven in educational circles throughout the nation will be marked as a year of celebration in his honor; and

Whereas, It is highly fitting that this commonwealth express its appreciation of Horace Mann and his distinguished service and devotion to the public service and to the cause of education; therefore be it

Resolved, That the governor is hereby requested to set apart a day during the current year, to be designated Horace Mann Day, and issue a proclamation recommending that said day be observed by the people with appropriate exercises in the public schools and otherwise commemorative of the life and work of said Horace Mann.

Approved April 6, 1937.

The Commonwealth of Massachusetts

By His Excellency
CHARLES F. HURLEY
Governor

A PROCLAMATION
1937

This year marks the one hundredth anniversary of the establishment of the

MASSACHUSETTS BOARD OF EDUCATION

which preceded for eighty-two years the present Department of Education, and the appointment of

HORACE MANN

as the first Secretary to that Board, which office is now designated as Commissioner of Education.

The Board was set up to guide, and by persuasion, through those in charge of education, to assist us in preserving the traditions of self-government established by the forefathers of this Commonwealth.

As pioneer Secretary of this first Board of Education, Horace Mann discharged his responsibility in a manner to win immortal honor for himself and his work in this State. The public schools of Massachusetts and of America owe much of their advancement to Horace Mann.

Therefore, I, Charles F. Hurley, Governor of the Commonwealth of Massachusetts, proclaim May 4th as Horace Mann Day, and suggest that on this day and during the period May 1st through November 30th of this year, proper time be set aside and appropriate ways be devised by the schools and libraries of the State for carrying the story of Horace Mann and his work to all our citizens.

"If ever there was a cause, if ever there can be a cause, worthy to be upheld by all of toil or sacrifice that the human heart can endure, it is the cause of education."

Given at the Executive Chamber, in Boston, this Twentieth day of April, in the year of our Lord one thousand nine hundred and thirty-seven, and of the Independence of the United States of America the one hundred and sixty-first.

CHARLES F. HURLEY.

By His Excellency the Governor,
FREDERICK W. COOK,
Secretary of the Commonwealth

GOD SAVE THE COMMONWEALTH OF MASSACHUSETTS

FOREWORD

In issuing this commemorative volume . . .

FOREWORD

In issuing this commemorative volume for use in the schools of this Commonwealth, and as a successor in the great office created by the Legislature and inspired by Horace Mann's Secretaryship, I am pleased to place as my foreword to the publication the final words of Horace Mann's last address to the graduating class at Antioch College in 1859:

"I beseech you to treasure up in your hearts these my parting words: be ashamed to die until you have won some victory for humanity."

Horace Mann's particular victory for humanity was to make "the dead letter of Massachusetts school law live in classrooms and community intelligence . . . " His faith in education and his courageous yet patient struggle in that cause won increased educational opportunity not only for the youth of Massachusetts, but also for the youth of the Nation.

May this volume, through the schools which he helped to found and the pupils for whom he helped to secure their present opportunities, serve well in carrying the story of Horace Mann and his work to all our citizens.

James G. Reardon

Commissioner of Education
Commonwealth of Massachusetts

COMMITTEE ON PREPARATION OF
HORACE MANN CENTENNIAL PAMPHLET

WILLIAM J. BARRY   *Chairman*:
Sub-master, Solomon Lewenberg School, Mattapan. Professor of History, Boston College Graduate School of Education.

JENNIE E. SCOLLEY   *Vice-Chairman*:
Ex-Assistant Superintendent of Schools, Holyoke.

ROBERT O. SMALL   *Secretary*:
Director of Vocational Education, Massachusetts Department of Education.

HERBERT H. HOWES   *Executive Committee*:
President, Hyannis State Teachers College.

FREDERICK W. PORTER   *Executive Committee*:
Superintendent of Schools, Greenfield.

THOMAS F. POWER   *Executive Committee*:
Assistant Superintendent of Schools, Worcester.

CHESTER R. STACY   *Executive Committee*:
Superintendent of Schools, Brewster, Dennis, Yarmouth.

NORMAN D. BAILEY   Superintendent of Schools, Berkley, Dighton, Freetown, Gosnold.

J. STEARNS CUSHING   Superintendent of Schools, Middleborough.

J. FRANKLIN FARRELL   Superintendent of Schools, Adams.

FLAVEL M. GIFFORD   Superintendent of Schools, Holliston, Medway, Sherborn.

LINCOLN D. LYNCH   Superintendent of Schools, Norwood.

MARTIN F. O'CONNOR   President, Framingham State Teachers College.

BERT J. LOEWENBERG   Assistant State Director, Federal Writers' Projects, Works Progress Administration.

Horace Mann on the Rostrum, as President of the
Massachusetts Senate

LEGISLATIVE ACT CREATING
THE MASSACHUSETTS BOARD OF EDUCATION

BE it enacted . . .

LEGISLATIVE ACT CREATING THE MASSACHUSETTS BOARD OF EDUCATION
1837

Chap. CCXLI.
An Act Relating to Common Schools.

BE it enacted by the Senate and House of Representatives, in General Court assembled, and by the authority of the same, as follows:

SEC. 1. His Excellency the Governor with the advice and consent of the Council, is hereby authorized to appoint eight persons, who together with the governor and lieutenant governor ex officiis, shall constitute and be denominated the Board of Education; and the persons, so appointed shall hold their offices, for the term of eight years: provided, the first person named in said board shall go out of office at the end of one year, the person next named, shall go out of office at the end of two years, and so of the remaining members, one retiring each year and in the order in which they are named, till the whole board be changed, and the governor with the advice and consent of the council as aforesaid, shall fill all vacancies in said board, which may occur from death, resignation or otherwise.

SEC. 2. The board of education, shall prepare and lay before the legislature in a printed form on or before the second Wednesday of January annually, an abstract of the school returns received by the secretary of the Commonwealth, and the said board of education, may appoint their own secretary, who shall receive a reasonable compensation for his services not exceeding one thousand dollars per annum, and who shall under the direction of the board collect information of the actual condition and efficiency of the common schools and other means of popular education; and diffuse as widely as possible throughout every part of the Commonwealth, information of the most approved and successful methods of arranging the studies and conducting the education of the young, to the end that all children in this Commonwealth, who depend upon common schools for instruction, may have the best education which those schools can be made to impart.

SEC. 3.   The board of education annually, shall make a detailed report to the legislature of all its doings, with such observations, as their experience and reflection may suggest upon the condition and efficiency of our system of popular education, and the most practicable means of improving and extending it.

SEC. 4.   For the salary of the secretary of the board of education, provided for in the second section of this act, the governor is authorized to draw his warrants from time to time, as the same may be required.

Approved by the Governor, April 20, 1837.

LETTER OF ACCEPTANCE OF SECRETARYSHIP

I received your communication . . .

Boston   June 30th, 1837.

To His Honor George Hull & the
    Rev. Emerson Davis.

        Gentlemen,

                I received your com-
munication last evening, informing
me that I had been elected their Secretary by the Board of Education. I accept
the Office with gratitude, but, at the same
time, with such a consciousness of my
inadequacy, as inspires me with the
most strenuous desire that the Board
will give me their constant guidance
& cooperation in the discharge of its duties.

        Be pleased, Gentlemen, to make known
to the Board, my sincere acknowledgments
for this testimonial of their favor, & to
accept for them & for yourselves the as-
surances of my respect & esteem,

                Horace Mann

His Honor Geo. Hull & the Rev. Emerson Davis./Com-tee.

To His Honor George Hull
& Rev. Emerson Davis.

30th—June   1837   H. Mann

Accepting the Office of
Secretary

LETTER OF RESIGNATION FROM SECRETARYSHIP

By the By-laws of the Board of Education . . .

Washington, D. C.   May 20th, 1848.

To His Excellency,

        Governor Briggs.

Chairman of the Board of Education.

        Dear Sir,

            By the By-laws of the Board of Education, its next annual meeting will be held at the Council Chamber in Boston, on Wednesday, the 31st inst., commencing at 10 cl'k. A. M. From this meeting, I xpect to be una-voidably detained; but I have left the Record-book of the Board, & the files of its papers in the hands of the Hon. Wm. B. Calhoun, Secretary of State, to be deliver-ed to the Board at its meeting.

        The ensuing will be the Twelfth Annual Meeting of the Board. At each of its preceding meetings, I have had the pleasure to be present; at each, I have had the honor to be elected as Secretary of this Honorable Body.

For these successive reelections, I feel it to be
impossible sufficiently to xpress my gratitude; for they have conferred upon me the only
office I ever coveted, & have placed me in
direct & active relation to the only object of
ambition I have ever had,--the well-being
of <u>all</u> the people, thro' the instrumentality of
education. To have had an opportunity to labor in
this cause, thro' such a series of years, I
regard as the happiness of my life; & tho'
this happiness has not been without its
trials, yet I am sure that the pain of the
trials will pass away, while the remem-
brance of the joy will survive & abide.
I had long cherished the hope, that, either
in a public or a private capacity, I might
remain in this field of labor during the
residue of my life; but since the last meeting of the Board, circumstances have in-
tervened, which will, partially & temporarily at least,
divert me from this immedi-
ate work. My hands may be taken from
it; but not my heart. My direct efforts
may be withdrawn from it; but my interest in it can never be alienated. Among benevolent objects, it is the most benevolent; a-

mong noble pursuits, it is the noblest; a-
mong objects of ambition, I regard it as the highest.

As present engagements, however, in another
sphere, will render it impossible for me to perform all the duties of the Secretaryship, thro'
the ensuing year, I must decline a reelec-
tion; & I beg you to communicate this, my
intention, to the Board.

In dissolving my official relation-
ship with a body of gentlemen, under
whom & with whom, I have so long la-
bored, in striving to secure & to advance
the dearest interests of the call, I cannot
take my leave without assuring them
of my gratitude for their long-contin-
ued kindness & support; nor without
xpressing the confident hope, that they
will be enabled, under the blessings of Divine Providence, to carry forward a
work which, so far, has not been pros-
ecuted without some reward for past
labors, & some encouragement for continued xertions.

And to you, Sir, in an especial
manner, do I feel myself under obliga-

tions; because, amid all the duties & the
dignities of your official position, you
have ever been mindful of the great
truth, that the highest of all duties & the
most xalted of all dignities, consists in
ransoming our fellow-beings from the
degradation of ignorance & vice, & in se-
curing the universal spread & the triumphant ascendancy of intelligence
& virtue.

     With deep sentiments of respect for
yourself, & your colleagues on the Board,
I am, dear Sir, very truly yours & their
friend & servant.

                         Horace Mann,
          Secy. of the Bd. of Education.

PREFACE

The Committee on the Horace Mann Centennial . . .

PREFACE

The Committee on the Horace Mann Centennial offers this pamphlet as a memorial to the life and educational accomplishments of Horace Mann. The year 1937 should be of interest to all residents of the United States and of particular interest to those of the Commonwealth of Massachusetts. This year marks the one hundredth anniversary of the appointment of Horace Mann as the first Secretary of the Board of Education of Massachusetts. With the purpose of honoring the memory of this great educator and of promoting an understanding and appreciation of the great debt succeeding generations owe him for his part in the founding of the great common schools of our state, Commissioner of Education James G. Reardon has recommended that schools, colleges, and citizen groups commemorate this anniversary during the year 1937.

Herein is subject matter which teachers will find appropriate for programs planned to observe that anniversary. In the table of contents, teachers from primary grades through senior high schools will find material which may be adapted to class or school programs. Material from which there may be developed exercises for school assemblies, graduation programs, radio programs, and commemorative programs will also be found therein. A bibliography has been organized for intensive work or special reports for use by pupils in the upper grades, senior high schools, and teachers colleges. We suggest that school officials bring the anniversary before local adult groups by availing themselves of such speakers as may be available.

The Committee respectfully submits this pamphlet as an expression of the State's recognition of the vision, wisdom, courage, and ability of Horace Mann in laying the foundation for equal opportunity in education in Massachusetts.

ACKNOWLEDGMENTS

It is a pleasure to give due credit to those who contributed so generously in one way or another to the preparation of this work. The Committee wish to express their sincere appreciation to:

Mrs. Blanche D. Sampson, Holyoke, for the Sonnet; Miss Marcella Rose Kelly, B. S., Holyoke, Miss Emily T. Thompson, A. B., Holyoke, and Edward S. Murphy, Student, Brockton High School, for the Pageants; Miss Louie G. Ramsdell, Framingham Teachers College, for the Biography; Miss Amy R. Whittier, Head, Department of Teacher-Training, and Miss Emma Porter Lennon, Instructor, Massachusetts School of Art, Miss Helen E. Cleaves, Director of Art, and Miss Margaret D. Stone, Supervisor of Art, Boston Public Schools, for their contributions to the Art Outline and Illustrations; and to Mr. Frank L. Allen, Supervisor, Vocational Art Education in Industry and Business, State Department of Education, for his direction and assistance in the art work; Mrs. Margaret Barberio, Senior Stenographer, for handling the correspondence; Miss Sophia Mankowich, Senior Stenographer, for typing the manuscript; and Miss Anna M. Murray, Head Clerk, Department of Education, for editing the manuscript.

The Committee is under special obligation to the following for their generous cooperation in furnishing information for the Bibliography:

Miss E. Kathleen Jones, General Secretary, and Miss Louise M. Alcott, Junior Assistant Librarian, both of the Division of Public Libraries, Department of Education.

The resources of the State Library were made available by State Librarian Dennis Dooley and Mrs. Barbara Smith, Senior Library Assistant, to whom we extend our grateful thanks.

Valuable assistance in a general way, both as to location of documents and buildings associated with Horace Mann, has been given by Albert T. Patty, Principal of the Franklin High School, Franklin, Massachusetts.

The Committee herewith acknowledges its appreciation of the services, in preparation of the pamphlet, of Dr. Bert J. Loewenberg, Assistant Director of the Federal Writers' Projects of Massachusetts under the Works Progress Administration.

View of Horace Mann's Birthplace, Mann's Plains,
Franklin, Massachusetts

BIOGRAPHY

BIOGRAPHY

Horace Mann . . .

HORACE MANN'S CONTRIBUTION TO EDUCATION

Horace Mann grew to manhood in a critical period for public school education in America. Although the early part of the nineteenth century was significant for its dynamic beginnings in the political and material development of the United States, the important problem of the education of the youth for the continuance of the democracy was, for the most part, ignored.

The rapidly increasing number of textile mills furnished wide opportunity for child labor; the cotton gin was fastening slavery in ever-increasing magnitude upon the South; the railroad and the steamboat were giving tremendous impetus to transportation and the consequent increase of production; the War of 1812 had settled, for a century at least, the question of the freedom of the seas; the promulgation of the Monroe Doctrine had turned backward any European interference in the New World; and the opening up of the great interior and western lands of the United States was calling for mighty effort and abundant means.

Public school education, however, the key to the enduring success of all political and industrial effort, was at a low ebb. State and citizens were apathetic to the situation. This type of education had had vital impetus given to it by Colonial legislation in Massachusetts. The Acts of 1642 and 1647 made provision for education for the children, first in the family and then in the elementary school; and in addition, had provided for a grammar school competent to fit young men for the university in towns of one hundred or more families. The Act of 1692 punished by heavy fines towns failing to make these required provisions for public school education.

In the days succeeding the Colonial Period and on through the first quarter of the nineteenth century, however, such was the indifference of the people and the State Legislature that the "system of free public schools in Massachusetts" had degenerated to "a leaderless chaos of between 1500 to 2500 one-room, ungraded, district schools, each in charge of a 'prudential committee' elected by the voters of the district." Frequently this committee consisted of one man who "chose the teacher, selected the textbooks, and otherwise managed the school." "In 1837 about 400 of the 2800 country winter schools were closed" because the teachers had been "put out" by the "unruly big boys — often older than the teacher himself, — who came for that purpose only." "The 5,600 teachers employed each year in the rural district schools of the state were a rapidly shifting group, busy most of the year in other occupations. Most of them had no education beyond" that which they had received in these same schools. "Many were incompetent; their only method of instruction was to compel memorization through fear of physical punishment." "All ideas that did not come from books were disclaimed by the teachers and any attempt at thought was rigidly suppressed." Because of this low status of education in the public school, leading citizens in many communities established private schools and academies for the training of their children. This in turn brought about even greater neglect of the common school.

In one of the poorest of these rural schools in the town of Franklin, Horace Mann spent the weeks devoted each year to his public school life. Although his parents were poor in material goods they were rich in the tradition of learning, of benevolence, and of high moral principle. His father died in 1809 when Horace was but thirteen. His mother, "a woman of superior intellect . . . and of rare force of character", of whom he was later to write, "She deserves my love for her excellence, and my gratitude for the thousand nameless kindnesses which she has ever, in the fulness of parental affection, bestowed upon me," was left with the care of three sons and a daughter. Already trained in farm work, Horace now gave all his time to the hard labor of the farm and the braiding of straw from the hat factory that he might assist his mother in keeping the home and the family. In a letter to a friend in later years he wrote of these days: "I believe in the rugged nursing of Toil; but she nursed me too much. In the winter time, I was employed in in-door and sedentary occupations, which confined me too strictly; and in summer, when I could work on the farm, the labor was too severe, and often encroached upon the hours of sleep. I do not remember the time when I began to work. Even my playdays — not play-days, for I never had any, but my play-hours — were earned by extra exertions, finishing tasks early to gain a little leisure for boyish sports . . . I have derived one compensation, however, from the rigor of my early lot. Industry, or diligence became my second nature; and I think it would puzzle any psychologist to tell where it joined on to the first. Owing to these ingrained habits, work has always been to me what water is to a fish. I have wondered a thousand times to hear people say, 'I don't like this business'; or 'I wish I could exchange for that'; for with me, whenever I have had anything to do, I do not remember ever to have demurred, but have always set about it like a fatalist; and it was as sure to be done as the sun is to set.

"Yet, with these obstructions, I had a love of knowledge which nothing could repress. An inward voice raised its plaint forever in my heart for something nobler and better; and, if my parents had not the means to give me knowledge, they intensified the love of it . . . I was taught to take care of the few books we had, as though there was something sacred about them. I never dog-eared one in my life, nor profanely scribbled upon title-pages, margin, or fly-leaf; and would as soon have stuck a pin through my flesh as through the pages of a book."

His vigorous youthful experiences led him to realize that knowledge was his "needed instrument". So he pursued knowledge. He eagerly read the hundred-odd books of history and theology which Benjamin Franklin had presented to the town of Franklin in acknowledgment of its having been named in his honor. In later years Mann stated, "Had I the power, I would scatter libraries over the whole land as the sower sows his wheatfield." In his further zealous quest for knowledge he prepared for Brown University in six months under the efficient guidance of Samuel Barrett, an itinerant but fine teacher of the classics.

He was admitted to the sophomore class of Brown University in September, 1816, at the age of twenty. He soon took first place in his own class and in the college. It is recorded of him that "he read the works of the Greek and Roman authors with ease, that he was proficient in the sciences, and that he was an able writer, debater, and orator." In one of his college themes entitled "The Duty of Every American to Posterity", he declared his attitude toward individual civic responsibility. Later in his commencement oration he announced his faith in the theory of the perfectability of the human race. Thus, even during his college career, he enunciated the ideal of service for humanity, the ideal which was to control the future years of his life.

In the year following his graduation he returned for a short period of time to Brown University as a successful tutor of Latin and Greek. His conduct of these early classes was characteristic of his later efforts for perfection in detail and in spirit. "He taught his Latin classes to look through the whole list of synonyms given in the Latin-English dictionary, and to select from among them all the one which would convey the author's idea, in the most expressive, graphic, and elegant manner, rendering military terms by military terms, nautical by nautical, the language of the rulers in language of majesty and command, of suppliants by words of entreaty, and so forth. This method improves diction surprisingly. The student can almost feel his organ of language grow under its training; at any rate, he can see from month to month that he has grown."

His Alma Mater remembers him not only as an impulsive, genial favorite of his classmates and as a modest, able student, but also as an attractive and inspiring teacher. As a member of the President's household, he met the President's daughter, Charlotte, whom he married in 1830, after having prepared for the practice of law.

Horace Mann studied law in Judge Gould's school in Litchfield, Connecticut. One of his classmates in the school writes of Mr. Mann's "massive brow and high arching head . . . his mild, bright eye, and the pleasant expression of the eloquent mouth" which "told of geniality and mirthfulness." This same classmate continues, "It was therefore easy to believe what was told me by the students, that he was the best fellow and the best in the office; but not before I formed his acquaintance was it so credible to me (what I was also told) that he was the best whist player, the best scholar, and the best lawyer of the school." At the end of the letter, the writer adds, "I parted from Mr. Mann at Litchfield, with the full conviction that his was to be one of the great names of our time. . . . The only drawback to the realization of such a destiny seemed to be the lack of physical vigor compared with the immense development of his nervous system. . . . His rich nervous temperament had, however, something of that wiry nature which gave the muscular and vital functions, as well as the mental, great capacity for endurance."

By 1823 Horace Mann was admitted to the Norfolk County bar and was established in the law office of Honorable James Richardson of Dedham, Massachusetts. During his brief career as a lawyer he is said to have gained "at least four out of five of all the contested cases in which he was engaged. The inflexible rule of his professional life was never to undertake a case that he did not believe to be right. He held that an advocate loses his highest power when he loses the ever-conscious conviction that he is contending for the truth; that though the fees or fame may be a stimulus, yet that a conviction of being right is itself creative of power, and renders its possessor more than a match for antagonists otherwise greatly his superior. He used to say that in this conscious conviction of right there was a magnetism; and he only wanted an opportunity to be put in communication with a jury in order to impregnate them with his own belief." It was during this brief period of legal experience that he came to a realization that crime is a civic disease, that through the right kind of educational treatment criminals may be cured, and that the potential criminal may be guided into a respectable way of life. Thus, he carried into his work as a lawyer his ideal of the individual's civic responsibilities.

Because of his integrity of purpose and honesty of practice Horace Mann was elected to be the Representative of Dedham to the State Legislature in 1827. For ten years, either as Representative or as Senator, "humanitarian reforms — charities, benevolent institutions, temperance, religious liberty, morality, and education, commanded his entire thought and energy."

The sudden loss of his wife, Charlotte Messer Mann, in 1832, caused such deep sorrow to Mr. Mann that his friends feared for his future. Through their importunity he left Dedham for Boston, where he increasingly concentrated his energy upon his humanitarian work. During this period he grew into close friendship with Dr. Samuel G. Howe, "educator of the blind"; Dr. Channing, great Boston divine; Dorothea Dix, "pioneer in humane treatment of the insane"; Dr. Taylor, Father of the Sailor's Bethel; Charles Sumner, fervent opponent of slavery; and Dr. George Combe, the Scotch philosopher.

During his legislative career Horace Mann's work in the field of education was most important. A realization of the imperative need for changes in the educational practice of the state was growing slowly. Several people had been instrumental in bringing this need to public attention. In 1826, William Russell, editor of THE AMERICAN JOURNAL OF EDUCATION, had dedicated himself to "the promulgation of liberal ideas, the training of females and the furtherance of elementary education". This journal and its successor, THE AMERICAN ANNALS OF EDUCATION AND INSTRUCTION, devoted much space to foreign education, particularly to Pestalozzi, and to the collection of information on educational conditions both in America and in Europe. James G. Carter, a graduate of Harvard in 1820, and a teacher of a few years, published in 1824 an account of the educational conditions in the New England schools in the first quarter of the nineteenth century. He wrote of the necessity for immediate and thorough improvement in the public school system, and of the need for "providing training of competent teachers for these schools. He urged, further, the establishment of a state supported institution equipped with an appropriate library and 'philosophical apparatus' and in charge of a principal with assistant professors in the various departments. . . . Finally he suggested the establishment of a board of commissioners which should represent the public interest and reflect its wishes." A bill embodying these ideas failed to pass by one vote in the Legislative Session of 1827.

Mr. Carter again advocated a bill in 1837, entitled *An Act Relating to Common Schools.* This provided for a State Board of Education and the appointment of a secretary to be "reasonably compensated", whose duty was to collect information on the condition and efficiency of the common schools and to distribute information on the general subject of Education. Horace Mann, as President of the Massachusetts Senate, signed the bill on April 19, 1837.

The selection of Horace Mann as the first secretary of this Board of Education was furthered by Edmund Dwight, a prominent business man of Boston and also a member of the Board of Education. Mr. George B. Emerson, a contemporary Boston schoolmaster, believed that "the Board wisely chose for its executive officer a member of a profession so foreign to teaching that he would be able to consider every question from a new point of view. Furthermore, Mr. Mann held a prominent place in the State, and his mental and moral endorsements were pre-eminent." He also felt that "Mr. Mann's profound and intimate acquaintance with the laws and institutions of Massachusetts . . . (and) his strong humanitarian faith, feeling, and practice" eminently fitted him for the high position which had been conferred upon him. About seventy-five years later, in retrospect, Dr. Arthur Norton of Harvard University wrote, "Few persons in Massachusetts saw as did Mann the responsibilities and opportunities of the new post."

In discussing his acceptance of the secretaryship, Horace

Mann declared, "Henceforth so long as I hold this office, I devote myself to the supremest welfare of mankind upon earth." To the pages of his journal, on July 18, 1837, he confided his hopes, "Could I be assured that my efforts in this new field of labor would be crowned with success, I know of no occupation that would be more agreeable to me, more congenial to my tastes and feelings. It presents duties entirely accordant with my principle. . . . If I can be the means of ascertaining what is the best construction of houses, what are the best books, and what is the best arrangement of studies, what are the best modes of instruction, if I can discover by what appliance of means a non-thinking, non-reflecting, non-speaking child can most surely be trained into a noble citizen ready to contend for the right and to die for the right — if I can only obtain and diffuse throughout this state a few good ideas on these and similar subjects, may I not flatter myself that my ministry has not been wholly in vain?"

Horace Mann's first efforts in his new task were directed toward the awakening of the public conscience to the need of better buildings and higher standards of common school education. This was the theme of his first lecture tour through the state. Now, from 1815 on, a better educational system had been advocated by a group of progressive Massachusetts thinkers — George Ticknor, George Bancroft, Edward Everett, and Charles Brooks, out of their interest in the German school system and in the doctrines of Pestalozzi. In response, therefore, to these newer ideas of education, Edmund Dwight pledged the sum of $10,000 for the establishment of Teachers Seminaries if the Commonwealth would provide a like amount; and on a second tour of the state, in the fall of 1838, Mr. Mann emphasized the need of special preparation for teachers in Normal Schools by his lecture entitled "Special Preparation a Prerequisite for Teaching" in order to gain the necessary legislative action.

In making known to the Massachusetts Legislature the proposition of Edmund Dwight for the establishment of Teachers Seminaries, Mr. Mann wrote, "as this proposal comprehends the whole of the rising generation in its philanthropic plan, I cannot refrain from earnestly soliciting for it the favorable regards of the Legislature." It is a fact of some significance that Governor Everett signed this bill of such importance for a democracy on April 19, 1838, an anniversary day famous throughout the country.

After long consideration as to the best means of providing teacher preparation, the Board decided to establish three normal schools, each in a different section of the state. The first one, "for females only", was opened at Lexington on July 3, 1839, under the leadership of Cyrus Peirce of Waltham, an inspiring teacher in Nantucket schools during the heyday of its prosperity in the whaling business. This first school was later moved to West Newton in 1844 and finally to Framingham in 1853. The second normal school, for the training of both men and women teachers, was opened at Barre, September 4, 1839, and later moved to Westfield. The third school, which has remained in its original location, was opened at Bridgewater, September 9, 1840.

Perhaps the establishment of these three schools and their development in those critical days is the greatest memorial of Horace Mann's twelve years of service as Secretary of the Massachusetts Board of Education, for they were the pioneer public schools for the training of teachers in the United States.

In the effort to accomplish his work as Secretary, Mr. Mann not only greatly concerned himself with the welfare of the normal schools, but he conducted series of lectures in the several counties of the state on the different phases of education for conventions of teachers and other interested people. He also edited the semi-monthly COMMON SCHOOL JOURNAL for the furtherance of knowledge concerning the management of schools and methods of teaching.

Two additional phases of school work next aroused his ardent efforts — the school library as an invaluable asset to the child and the teacher, and the institute as a "provision for the better qualification" of teachers. Concerning the school library and the institute, Mr. Mann wrote to the Board of Education in

1844, "We have borrowed her (New York's) system of school libraries, let us now adopt the system of teachers' institutes which she has projected, and thus maintain that noble rivalry of benefactions which is born of philanthropy." Again Edmund Dwight generously provided $1,000 for experimentation in this new work of the teachers' institute.

As a method of summarizing his accomplishments in education and of presenting his ideas for further progress, Horace Mann made, year by year, reports to the State Board of Education. There are twelve such "Annual Reports", which are treasured today by all educators as remarkable educational documents. It is his "Seventh Report", containing his personal observations on the high standards of the European school system, which is the most famous because it aroused a group of more or less poorly prepared Boston schoolmasters to protest against its suggestions for improving the schools of Massachusetts. The "Twelfth Report", made in 1848 after he had resigned his post in order to go as Representative to Washington, contains a summary of his work and of the progress made by the common schools of Massachusetts during the twelve years of his secretaryship. All the reports were published in the COMMON SCHOOL JOURNAL, which had a wide circulation throughout the country. Of these reports George B. Emerson wrote, "They have already reached beyond the limits of our narrow State. In the remotest corner of Ohio forty men, not children and women, but men, meet together to read aloud a single copy of the Secretary's Reports which one of them receives; thousands of the best friends of humanity of all sects, parties and creeds in every state in the Union are familiar with the name of Horace Mann."

In 1843, while still Secretary, Mr. Mann married Mary Peabody of the Peabody family of Salem. Together they visited and studied the schools of Europe to bring back new inspiration for the schools of the Commonwealth. This study furnished the materials for the Seventh Annual Report.

Mr. Mann's career in Washington extended over a period of four years, 1848 – 1852. He was chosen to fill the vacancy caused by the death of Representative John Quincy Adams, and then was reelected for two terms. Being greatly interested in the freeing of the slaves and yet feeling that he could not enter into this political question without detriment to educational matters while he was still Secretary of the Board of Education, he welcomed the opportunity to give up his work in Massachusetts.

A section from his letter to his Scottish friends, Mr. and Mrs. Combe, written on November 15, 1850, gives in his own words the reasons for his decision to accept the Washington post: "When first offered the nomination for Congress, I had serious doubts about accepting it: but I was in my twelfth year as Secretary of the Board of Education; and, while acting in an official capacity, I was under the trammels of neutrality between all sects and parties. It was just at the crisis when the destiny of our new Territory of about six hundred thousand square miles in extent was about to be determined. All of human history that I ever knew respecting the contest for political and religious freedom, and my own twelve-years' struggle to imbue the public mind with an understanding not merely of the law but of the spirit of religious liberty, had so magnified in my mind the importance of free institutions, and so intensified my horror of all forms of slavery, that even the importance of education itself seemed for a moment to be eclipsed.

"Besides, my fidelity to principles had made some enemies, who, to thwart me, would resist progress, but who, if I were out of the way, would be disarmed, and would co-operate where they had combated."

He hoped that the new duties would allow him some chance to recover his health which at great personal sacrifice he had utterly neglected for a long time in his eagerness to do everything possible to improve the educational conditions of Massachusetts. In the office of Representative he also saw a chance of working for the larger humanitarian interests and a possible chance of bringing about the establishment of a national education bureau for the furtherance of education in the United

States. This last, however, he failed to accomplish. All national thought at this time centered about the great controversy over slavery.

The intensity of Mr. Mann's feeling concerning slavery may be judged by his controversy with his Congressional colleague, Daniel Webster. Mr. Mann, as well as many other Massachusetts people, felt that Mr. Webster, by his advocacy of the Compromise Bill, had sacrificed the great principles of "freedom and truth for party, or political or personal considerations." So bitterly did Mr. Mann regret Webster's attitude that to a friend concerning the affair he said, "he (Webster) is a fallen star! Lucifer descended from heaven!"

Mr. Mann made five speeches in Congress. One of these, in opposition to the Fugitive Slave Act, was described by Henry Wilson, Representative from Natick, Massachusetts, as "one of the most brilliant speeches for liberty that ever fell from human lips."

In 1852, while a nominee for the office of Governor of Massachusetts, Horace Mann received an invitation to the presidency of Antioch College in Yellow Springs, Ohio. At that time Antioch College was just being organized and the thought of molding a new coeducational institution according to his educational ideas appealed to him greatly. He accepted the presidency with great enthusiasm and moved west with his family in September, 1852. In his entire administration of the college through the difficult days of its pioneer period Mr. Mann worked for three goals — to secure educational opportunities for women equal to those for men; to grant college degrees only to those students who proved worthy in personal living as well as in academic merit; to gain the best good for every member of the college by student cooperation and individual responsibility. He made it the first college in non-discrimination against color or race. He refused his sanction to any system of prizes for work well done.

As president of the college he "strove to make the acquaintance and gain the confidence of every student, and to impart to him his own inspiration to live for the highest ends." His successor in the presidency declared that it was the high ideals of the college imparted to its students by Horace Mann that made him wish to be its next leader.

The physical hardships of the pioneer life, the financial difficulties of the college, the lack of cooperation of the founders of the college, the great burden of the administrative duties added to the heavy teaching and preaching program which he undertook for the good of the institution, all served to break down the health of this great man. He died August 2, 1859, after six years of the most arduous, persistent, and zealous labor. But he had succeeded in placing Antioch College on a firm foundation of the most progressive type of modern education. His last words to his students were, "Treasure up in your hearts these my parting words: Be ashamed to die until you have won some victory for humanity." And these words were cut on his monument placed on the college campus.

Horace Mann's firm belief in the perfectability of the human race and his vision of a people well on the way toward that perfectability set his ideals high for the common school system not only of his own state of Massachusetts but of the entire nation — a common school system which should have a fine physical and intellectual status entirely unaffected by all religious and political controversies of the time. His vision for a happy, intelligent people included education for the blind, hospitals for the insane, opportunity for the negro equal to that of the white, and college opportunities where those of all classes, color, creed, and race might have abundant opportunity for growth in character, scholarship, and service to mankind.

In the face of grave difficulties he was able through these ideals to bring about a great educational revival. "Neither time nor care", he had said, "nor such thought as I am to originate, shall be wanting to make this an era in the welfare and prosperity of our schools; and, if it is so, it will be an era in the welfare of mankind."

As a result of his indefatigable and inspired labor, the common schools were "better-supported, better-taught, better-equipped"; teachers were given better preparation; normal training schools were established; teachers' institutes were inaugurated; the school year was "increased by one month"; school libraries were started; the curriculum was enriched; and "a spirit of educational enthusiasm" spread among the people and a strong "professional spirit arose among the teachers." Mr. Mann also brought about increased appropriations for the common schools, increased wages for both men and women teachers, an increase in the number of women teachers, an increase in school attendance, the compulsory "compensation for school supervision", and the establishment of fifty new high schools. These sweeping reforms in common schools and the founding of the high schools caused a lessening of the influence of the undemocratic private school.

In addition, Mr. Mann succeeded in demonstrating the practicability of his ideals for education and his power as a teacher in the firm foundation he gave to Antioch College in spite of all the petty, the grave, the academic, the physical, and the financial difficulties of his task.

Horace Mann's ideals and his accomplishments are his enduring monument, which today, a century later, are still quickening the educational thought.

Note: Those interested in a chronological listing of the principal events in the life of Horace Mann, and, in need of a source from which a more extensive biographical knowledge can be secured, will find help in the section devoted to the Bibliography.

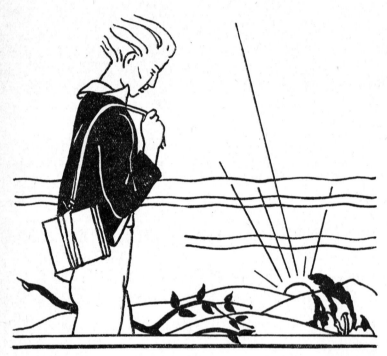

"How often when a boy did I stop to gaze at the glorious sunset . . ."

QUOTATIONS

QUOTATIONS

"If ever there be a cause . . . "

QUOTATIONS FROM HORACE MANN

"If ever there be a cause, if ever there can be a cause worthy to be upheld by all toil or sacrifice that the human heart can endure, it is the cause of education."

"If I can discover by what appliance of means a non-thinking, non-reflecting, non-speaking child can be most easily trained into a noble citizen ready to contend for the right and to die for the right — may I not flatter myself that my ministry may not be wholly in vain?"

"The common school is the institution which can receive and train up children in the elements of all good knowledge and of virtue, before they are submitted to the alienating competitions of life — the common school is the greatest discovery ever made by man."

"This country has been created on a splendid scale of physical magnificence. Are its intellectual and moral proportions to be of a corresponding greatness?"

"A man must know his faculties: he must know the subordination of the lower to the higher, and his practice must accord with his knowledge."

"Every day of my life impresses the conviction upon me more and more, how important is the early direction given to the sentiments as well as to the intellect."

"In this government it is not tolerable for any man, however high, or for any body of men, however large, to prescribe what subjects may be agitated, and what may not be agitated. I hold treason against this government to be an enormous crime; but great as it is, I hold treason against free speech to be incomparably greater."

"I can conceive no emotions more pure, more holy, more like those that glow in the bosom of a perfected being, than those which a virtuous son must feel towards an affectionate mother."

"When will society, like a mother, take care of *all* her children?"

"The individual who does not feel love is bereft of a source of unfailing happiness."

"Love is a universal solvent. Wilfulness will maintain itself against persecution, torture, death, but will be fused and dissipated by kindness, forbearance and sympathy. Here is a clew given by God to lead us through the labyrinths of the world."

"Henceforth I devote myself to the highest welfare of mankind upon earth."

"When will the human mind be instructed to arrange things upon a scale according to their intrinsic value, so as for the future to refuse the precedence to trivial and transitory objects over universal and immortal interests?"

"If the powers of the human mind and the resources of wealth were directed to ameliorate the condition of the unfortunate and afflicted, what a different world this would be!"

"I know one thing — if I stand by the principles of truth and duty, nothing can inflict upon me any permanent harm."

"God grant me an annihilation of selfishness, a mind of wisdom, a heart of benevolence."

"I have faith in the improvability of the race — in their accelerating improvability."

"There is a natural language which communicates to one mind the state or condition of another mind. In the language, words and sentences are subordinate instruments. Soul speaks to soul."

"Let the next generation, then, be my client."

"The time that comes to us is soft, yielding, like wax; we can shape it as we please."

"Mine may be the labor, and another's the honor. Well, if I knew the work would go on when my labors cease, I would not touch the question of ultimate honor."

"I will try to conquer, but if conquest be impossible, then I will try to bear."

"A spirit mildly devoting itself to a good cause is a certain conqueror."

"Be ashamed to die until you have won some victory for humanity."

"It is my belief that hereafter each individual will remember all that he has ever done, said, or thought. That is the book of judgment. May that volume be so filled that it may in after periods of existence be unrolled and examined with pleasure."

"The longer the youthful faith in goodness is fed, the better."

"We want no men who will change, like the vanes of our steeples, with the course of the popular wind; but we want men who, like mountains, will change the course of the wind."

"There is now power enough among the educated men of the country to save it, if that power were rightly used."

"I feel none the less inclined to discuss the question of freedom because an order has gone forth that it shall not be discussed. Discussion has been denounced as agitation, and then it has been dictatorially proclaimed that 'agitation must be put down'. Humble as I am, I submit to no such dictation, come from what quarter or what numbers it may. If such a prohibition is intended to be laid upon me personally, I repel it. If intended to silence me as the representative of the convictions and feelings of my constituents, I repel it all the more vehemently."

"As shadows are always deepest where light is brightest, those who are in the shadows of the brightest light of civilization are in the deepest darkness."

"Had I the power, I would scatter libraries over the whole land as the sower sows his wheat field."

"Let education, then, teach children this great truth — that God has so constituted this world, into which He has sent them, that whatever is really and truly valuable may be possessed by all, and possessed in exhaustless abundance."

"However, after all the advice which all the sages who ever lived could give, there is no security against danger, and in favor of success, as to undertake it with a right spirit — with a self-sacrificing spirit. Man can resist influence of talent; they

will deny demonstration, if need be; but few will combat
goodness for any length of time."

"The generous and impartial mind does not ask whence it
comes, but what is it."

"All my boyish castles in the air had references to doing
something for the benefit of mankind."

SUGGESTIVE WAYS FOR OBSERVANCES TO BE
ADAPTED FOR COMMON SCHOOLS, HIGH SCHOOLS,
TEACHERS COLLEGES, AND CITIZEN GROUPS

Pageants
Units of Work
Topics for Special Reports or Individual Projects
Composition Work
Art Work
Radio Programs
Planting Horace Mann Tree
Hanging Horace Mann Picture

PAGEANTS

1. YON GOLDEN KEYS

   A Portrait and Prayer Dedicated to Horace Mann, Father of Common School Education in Massachusetts, On the Occasion of the Massachusetts Centennial In His Honor.

   For Elementary and Junior High School Presentation.

   By

   Marcella Rose Kelly, B. S., Holyoke.

2. FATHER OF FREE PUBLIC SCHOOLS

   A Pageant Depicting Mann's Life at Brown University, His Public Life in Dedham and in the Legislature, Establishment of Board of Education with Horace Mann as Secretary, Establishment of First Public Normal Schools, Mann's Trip to Europe and Criticism of Boston Schools, 1817–1853.

   For Junior and Senior High School Presentation.

   By

   Edward S. Murphy, Student, Brockton High School.

3. THE GREAT CRUSADER

   Horace Mann in Symbolic Pageantry

   For Presentation by Senior High Schools, Teachers Colleges, and Citizen Groups.

   By

   Emily T. Thompson, A. B., Holyoke.

YON GOLDEN KEYS

A Portrait and Prayer Dedicated to Horace Mann,
Father of Common School Education in Massachusetts,
on the Occasion of the Massachusetts Centennial
in His Honor

1937

A Pageant

For Elementary and Junior High School Presentation

By
Marcella Rose Kelly, B. S.,
Holyoke, Massachusetts

YON GOLDEN KEYS

Education, religious and political freedom . . .

"Education, religious and political freedom, then, were the watchwords of his life and actions. All collateral evils would vanish if these things could be established. In one sense, he cannot be said to have sacrificed himself to them; for he identified himself with them, and cared little for anything else. To work for them was his happiness.

"Mr. Mann felt that the vocation of educator was the highest possible one in a republic. He approached it with the deepest awe and a sense of the highest responsibility, gladly relinquishing senatorial honors and wealth for its arduous and interesting duties."

— From *"Life and Works of Horace Mann by His Wife"*

YON GOLDEN KEYS

Episodes

Sets Required

Four interiors and one exterior.
All sets may be revised to meet individual problems of staging.

Costumes Used

Pre-Civil War costumes with the exception of Prelude to Episode I and the last Episode, Episode V.

Properties

Properties are simple and enumerated in the introduction to each Episode.

Presentation

May be presented in the open or in an auditorium.

Music Required

No specific music has been mentioned. Types of orchestration to introduce each Episode is left to the discretion of the director.

YON GOLDEN KEYS

Prelude to Episode I

CHARACTERS

A POLICE OFFICER
A LITTLE BOY (ABOUT 10 YEARS OLD)
ENOUGH PEOPLE FOR A STREET SCENE
(These to be taken from upper elementary and junior high school grades)

BEFORE CURTAIN

[*On stage center, in front of drawn curtain stands a policeman going through all the pantomimic motions of traffic direction. He may have a whistle which he blows occasionally and at those times when he is not otherwise engaged in the manipulation of his hands — in signaling. In response to his directions, groups of people move left and right across stage center to disappear behind stage curtains at left and right of stage. It is to be understood that these groups come up from the audience by means of steps on each side of the stage. While this traffic is in motion, an orchestra or piano plays some brilliant, fast moving march that is militant in nature. After several groups have passed across stage and have disappeared behind draperies, one lone youngster, a little boy of ten or thereabouts, crosses from stage left to stage center, and addresses the officer on duty. At this point, the music is brought to a temporary halt.*]

LITTLE BOY.　Officer?

OFFICER.　Yes, youngster? What can I do for you?

LITTLE BOY.　[*Half-hesitantly*]　I b-beg your pardon, Sir, but is there a celebration or something somewhere around here?

OFFICER.　[*Astonished*]　Is there a celebration?　[*Now a tone higher*] IS THERE A CELEBRATION?　I should say there certainly is. Don't you go to school, youngster?

LITTLE BOY.　Yes, Sir. That is — I did, Sir.

OFFICER.　[*Kindly, but not following the lad*] You mean you did, or you do?

LITTLE BOY.　I did, officer. You see, I just moved into this state today. I do not begin school here until tomorrow.

OFFICER.   I see. Well, youngster, you walk right along down the street here, turn right, walk along for several blocks, and you will come to a large park. There, if you hurry along, you will find a pageant being presented.

LITTLE BOY.   A pageant?

OFFICER.   Yes. A kind of play called, Yon Golden Keys. The school children are presenting it in honor of HORACE MANN.

LITTLE BOY.   HORACE MANN? Who was he?

OFFICER.   He was the Father of Common School Education in Massachusetts. This year, this state into which you have just moved is celebrating his one hundredth anniversary. We call it, THE HORACE MANN CENTENNIAL.

LITTLE BOY.   [*Music again bursts forth*] And that's what the music is for?

OFFICER.   Yes, my lad, and if you don't hurry along, you won't get a seat.

LITTLE BOY.   Thank you, officer. Thank you. I'll run right along.

OFFICER.   [*Directing more moving traffic*] Move along, people. Step lively. This way to the HORACE MANN CENTENNIAL. Down this street, turn to your right, and walk along several blocks. Celebration at City Park. THIS WAY TO THE HORACE MANN CENTENNIAL!

[*Here the orchestra plays a resolving chord: a black fade-out in which the auditorium and stage are darkened completely for a moment to mark the transition between the Prelude and Episode I.*]

END OF PRELUDE

EPISODE I
Horace Mann — His Youth at Franklin, Mass.

CHARACTERS

MOTHER MANN
HER DAUGHTER
HER SON, HORACE [*age of nineteen — a tall
boy might portray Horace at this stage*]
MRS. EMMONS, *wife of the village Minister*

AT RISE OF CURTAIN

[*As the curtain rises, music of a simple, dignified, reverential nature is being played offstage. It ceases when the curtain has been fully drawn so that the characters may go into their dialogue.*

The stage setting is simple — a farmhouse dining-room, furnished after the fashion of most pre-Civil War dining rooms. At stage center is round dining-table at which are placed three chairs in readiness for use at the evening meal. At stage left, against the flat back of a plain setting, is a buffet characteristic of the period. At the right, opposite the buffet, is a cabinet for chinaware.

The costumes worn by the women are period costumes of the pre-Civil War era.

MOTHER MANN *is at stage center arranging dishes on the table.* HER DAUGHTER, *a youngster in her very early teens, is at stage right in the act of taking silver from the buffet drawer.* MOTHER MANN *opens the conversation.*]

MOTHER MANN.	Bring three forks and two more spoons, child.
DAUGHTER.	Yes, Mother.
MOTHER MANN.	Horace is later than usual this evening. I wonder what keeps him?
DAUGHTER.	What keeps him? [*Repeating what the mother says as if she well ought to know*] Work, Mother, of course. [*Pausing with silver in her hand*] Mother, why is it that Horace does nothing but work — work — work?
MOTHER.	We are humble farmer folk who must work to earn our daily bread. Our lot is different from most, my child. Your father died when your brother was thirteen. It's a man's lot that has fallen on his young shoulders.
DAUGHTER.	But surely, Mother, he ought to play more. When he finishes his work, he might play a little in his leisure hours.
MOTHER.	Your brother's leisure hours are few, I fear. Bring me that silver, girl. Now bring a butter knife. [*The child returns to the buffet for it.*]
DAUGHTER.	All the villagers say he is always down at Franklin Library pouring over musty old books.

MOTHER.	[*Leaving the stage center and going to china cabinet for more dishes.*] Hush, child! Your brother will some day be a great man. He has not always had the luck of the villagers. Until the age of fifteen, he had never had the chance to go to school more than eight or ten weeks in the year. And to think that now he is preparing for college!
DAUGHTER.	But the villagers say that he will get to be an old man before he knows it with his head always buried in groggy old Latin books and —
MOTHER.	I fear you are getting to be a gossip, child. Remember that gossip does not become a lady. And you must always be a lady, daughter.
DAUGHTER.	Yes, Mother. But studying — now I could never take to schooling like Horace does. Of course, I like to know what everybody in my classes knows, but ugh! [*Making a grimace*] I'd much rather make candy, pop corn, and have some fun when my daily work is done.
MOTHER.	Fun is all right in its place. But too much fun is worse than too little. [*A knock on the door*] Child, someone is knocking. See who may be at our door.
DAUGHTER.	[*Going to the door obediently*] Oh! Mrs. Emmons! Do come in! It's Mrs. Emmons, Mother.
MOTHER.	[*Pausing in the table arrangement*] Good evening, Mrs. Emmons. Do seat yourself here in this chair. [*Drawing a chair for her*].
MRS. EMMONS.	[*Seating herself*] Thank you, my dear.
MOTHER.	I was just completing preparations for our evening meal. We have to eat later than most folks hereabouts because Horace works longer in the fields than do most of the farmers.
MRS. EMMONS.	[*Understandingly*] Yes, I know. A wonderful boy, your son. I came at this awkward hour because I have some very happy news for him.
MOTHER.	[*Excitedly*] Good news for Horace?
MRS. EMMONS.	And such good news! [*Excited too*] Reverend Emmons received a communication from Brown University to the effect that your boy has passed the entrance examinations for which he studied so hard and so faithfully.
MOTHER.	Ah! How truly wonderful! It is the chance he has dreamed of for days.

Mrs. Emmons.	And well worthy is the lad of such an opportunity. Only yesterday, Minister Emmons was saying what a fine character the boy had. His faith in principle, his loyalty to duty, his gratitude for favors received, however small, and his affection for those who have stood by him, are remarkable traits in one whose years rest yet so lightly upon him.
Mother.	[*Dreamily*] His father was like that. And how proud he would have been of the lad. A humble farmer was his father, but he left with his son a strong impression of moral worth and an ingrained love of knowledge and truth.
Daughter.	[*From her place by the window where she has been standing during conversation between her mother and Mrs. Emmons*] Excuse me, Mother, but Horace is coming down the road now. When he hears this good news, he'll be so very happy.
Mrs. Emmons.	That he will, child. [*Speaking now to the Mother*] I'll go now, and leave you to impart to Horace the joyful news. And here [*handing her a document*] give this to the lad and have him affix his signature to it.
Mother.	[*Taking it*] Thank you, good friend. And thank Reverend Emmons for me, too.
Mrs. Emmons.	It is your son who deserves the praise and gratitude. His persevering efforts are responsible for that permit of entrance. Good night, my friend. My best wishes attend you.
Mother.	Good night, Mrs. Emmons.
Daughter.	Good night, Mrs. Emmons.
	[*Exit Mrs. Emmons*]
Daughter.	Oh, Mother! Horace is wonderful, isn't he? He succeeds in everything.
Mother.	That he does. Hard work never goes unrewarded. About your own work now, daughter, so that you may make the evening meal a treat for your brother.
Daughter.	Yes, Mother. I'll hasten to the kitchen at once and get the victuals.
Mother.	Do, child.
	[*Exit daughter*]
Horace.	[*Entering excitedly*] Oh, Mother! I met Mrs. Emmons as I came down the walk, and she told me to hasten here for there was news for me. Can it be . . . ??

MOTHER.	Yes, there is news, son. And such good news! What you have been wishing might happen. You have passed . . .
HORACE.	Passed the examinations for Brown University? Oh, Mother! How grand! How splendid! How wonderful — how wonderful!
MOTHER.	Yes, lad. Mrs. Emmons brought from the Reverence, her husband, this note of permit for you to sign. [*She hands it to him*].
HORACE.	[*Still excited*] I must sign it at once.
MOTHER.	The ink is there in the buffet drawer. You will find a quill-pen there, too. While you sign your name, lad, I'll attend to preparations for supper. It is almost in readiness.

·[*Exit, stage right*]

HORACE.	[*Getting pen and ink, and going back to the table, writes on the document reading aloud what he puts on the paper*] Horace Mann, born at Franklin, Massachusetts, on the fourth of May, 1796. [*Now he stands and takes stage center. He holds the document in his hand and speaks aloud in a slow, reverential voice.*] Now all my boyish castles in the air which have to do with the benefit of mankind will be realized, for I have a firm conviction that knowledge is my needed instrument. And I shall get that at Brown University. Brown University! Brown University!

[*As his voice trails off into nothingness on the last word, the curtain falls.*]

END OF EPISODE I

EPISODE II
Horace Mann — Lawyer, Statesman, Philanthropist

CHARACTERS

HORACE MANN, *Member of the Massachusetts*
    State Legislature
DR. WOODWARD ⎫
DR. TODD   ⎬ *All friends and colleagues*
MR. TAYLOR   ⎪   *of Mr. Mann*
MR. SUMNER   ⎭
CHAIRMAN OF HOUSE COMMITTEE
SEVERAL SENATORS

AT RISE OF CURTAIN

[*A militant march, played by the orchestra, ushers in the rise of stage curtain on Episode II. At full rise of curtain, music is brought to a halt and characters go into their dialogue.*

It is the year 1833. Mr. Horace Mann, renowned lawyer, and member of the Massachusetts State Legislature, is due on the floor. He is to make a speech on behalf of the Worcester Hospital for the Insane. Funds are needed for its completion; and as he sees it to be his duty, he is here in the HOUSE to fight for what he considers a cause worthy of the interests of all humanity.

The room in which members of the Legislature have assembled is a simple hall. At its stage center is a large desk draped in blue, white, and red. Above the desk on the flat back of the wall is a picture of Washington, also draped in blue, white, and red. Seated at the desk is a man, the chairman of the assembly. At his right is seated another man, the principal speaker of the gathering — MR. HORACE MANN. At the chairman's left is another chair for a young man, who, when the curtain rises, has evidently just finished his speech, for there is much applause from his audience as he takes the chair on the chairman's left. The audience consists of twelve men, assembled six on either side of the large desk. The seats for these members of the Legislature are arranged in semi-circular style.

The speaker on the left opens this episode. He is just finishing a speech when the curtain rises.]

DR. WOODWARD.   And we who are seated in this audience this morning are indeed the fortunate ones. It is we who should count our blessings. It is we who enjoy peace of soul, body and mind that should remember those less fortunate than ourselves. Those poor afflicted inmates of the Hospital for the Insane at Worcester need your support. They need more than your support. They need your prayers; they need your charity; they need the financial help which only your Legislature is empowered to give. For all these things, I have come before you this morning.

[*He seats himself next to the chairman; for a few minutes there is clapping of a semi-responsive nature.*]

MR. SUMNER. [*In the audience, in an aside to another auditor in the Legislature who is seated next him*] A good enough plea but wait until you hear the Honorable Mr. Mann.

DR. TODD. I have never had the honor of hearing the gentleman, but his name and fame are widespread not only in Massachusetts but even in the state of Connecticut. That is my home.

MR. SUMNER. Interesting, indeed. Some day his fame will be known from ocean to ocean, for there [*pointing to Mr. Mann who is conferring softly with the Chairman*] is the makings of a great, yes, a very great, leader.

MR. TAYLOR [*Seated next Mr. Sumner on his right*] True enough. I have known Mr. Mann a long time. He is a great orator. He speaks sincerely, too, and from the heart.

MR. SUMNER. The Chairman is rising. He must be about to present Mr. Mann now.

CHAIRMAN. Members of the Massachusetts State Legislature and honored guests, I present to you a man who needs no introduction to any of you, for his name and fame as a scholar, as a lawyer, and as a statesman have gone far afield. It was through his efforts in the beginning that the Hospital for the Insane at Worcester was established; it is on behalf of that same hospital that he wishes the floor to address you. The Honorable Mr. Mann.

[*There is much applause in the audience as the Honorable Mr. Mann rises to speak.*]

MR. MANN. Mr. Chairman, Dr. Woodward, fellow members of the Senate and friends. I am not going to make a speech. I am going to ask a question. Up at the Worcester Hospital for the Insane, there are two hundred-thirty human beings who live in darkness; they have eyes with which to see but their minds are ill and they see not; they have ears with which to hear but their minds are ill and they comprehend not; they have tongues with which to speak but their minds are ill and they speak not. I am here to ask the Legislature of Massachusetts to give its unanimous consent to the appropriation of $10,000 for the completion of the Hospital at Worcester so that these poor unfortunates, of whom my good friend, Dr. Woodward, spoke but a few moments before, might have a suitable place in which to live and in which to regain their mental health. The question rests with you for the answer.

[*Prolonged applause from the floor*]

FIRST SENATOR. Mr. Chairman?

CHAIRMAN. One moment, Senator, there is a question before the House. Does the Senate wish to appropriate the amount of money specified by Mr. Mann for the completion of the Worcester Hospital? All those in favor say, "Aye".

ALL. Aye! Aye! Aye!

CHAIRMAN. Those opposed? Say, "No", if there be any opposed.

[*No murmur of a voice in opposition*]

CHAIRMAN. [*Rapping on the desk with his gavel*] It is a vote that the State Legislature approves the appropriation of $10,000 for the purpose specified in Mr. Mann's motion. Now — if there be no further business, the meeting stands adjourned. [*He raps on his desk with gavel and the meeting adjourns.*]

[*Several men move forward to where Mr. Mann is seated and congratulate him on his efforts in behalf of the hospital.*]

DR. WOODWARD. A magnificent speech, friend.

MR. SUMNER. A fine plea for those less fortunate than ourselves.

MR. TAYLOR. A deed that will make you famous in years to come, Sir.

DR. TODD. I marvel at your ability to want a thing, to go after it, and to get it.

FIRST SENATOR. Congratulations, Sir. You are indeed a friend to those in need.

SECOND SENATOR. The legal profession, the state of Massachusetts, and the country at large have a great man in their midst.

MR. MANN. [*To all*] Gentlemen, you do me honor, but you have done greater honor to yourselves in appropriating to the good of these suffering fellow-beings of ours, $10,000. It must truly please the Creator when he sees humanity mindful of fellow brethren who are sometimes the more worthy, yet the less fortunate than themselves.

And as he stands there in the HOUSE saying these words of wisdom, soft music plays offstage and the curtain goes down.]

END OF EPISODE II

EPISODE III
Horace Mann — Teacher and Educator

CHARACTERS

HORACE MANN, *Teacher and Scholar*
DR. WOODWARD
MR. SUMNER

AT RISE OF CURTAIN

[*A slow, dignified type of music ushers in this Episode. The set required is simple. It is an interior — the law office of* MR. HORACE MANN, *lately elected Secretary of the Board of Education of Massachusetts.*

As the curtain rises, two men are seated on swivel chairs in Mr. Mann's law office. It is a dingy place that contains little furniture other than a desk, two chairs, and a book-case (which at the moment is empty of books). MR. MANN *is seated at the desk; his friend,* DR. WOODWARD, *is seated in the swivel chair to his right.*]

DR. WOODWARD. So — Horace, you are willing to sacrifice your fine practice in law to the cause of education?

MR. MANN. I am more than willing. I want to work for the young. As you see, from these empty book-cases here, I have no more intention of practicing my erstwhile profession.

DR. WOODWARD. And you feel certain, my friend, that there will be no regrets?

MR. MANN. I am quite certain there will be no regrets. The State of Massachusetts in appointing me to the high office of Secretary of the Board of Education has entrusted to me a noble task. I shall spend my life henceforward making myself worthy of the cause in which I have enlisted. I shall be mindful ever of the duties such a high office imposes upon me, I shall be loyal to its confidences, and I shall do all within my power to promote the welfare of all concerned within such a realm.

DR. WOODWARD. You disappoint me, Horace. I had hoped to see you become, as I know you could become, the greatest constitutional lawyer in the country.

MR. MANN. A good enough cause in itself, the law. But I know of no calling nobler, no work more edifying, no results more capable of enduring, than that which my new vocation does offer me. At the moment, I have one end in view and that is: I shall aim to raise the art of teaching to the dignity of a profession. I aim, too, to fight for common and equal educational opportunities for all.

Dr. Woodward.	You will meet with much discouragement.
Mr. Mann.	I go forth ready and willing to meet discouragement gladly; the cause is worth the fight at any cost.
Dr. Woodward.	If you truly feel that way, my friend, I rejoice in your decision, for I know the spirit of which you are made. I hear knocking at your door. Come in, Sir! [*this loudly so as to be heard from the inside*]
Mr. Sumner.	What's this I hear about you, Mr. Mann?
Mr. Mann.	Yes. Tell me what you hear about me. If it is truth, I will not deny it.
Mr. Sumner.	Why — they say in Boston that you are about to forfeit the cause of law to the cause of education. Is that true, Sir?
Mr. Mann.	True, Sir.
Mr. Sumner.	And they say that you are thinking of building not a school to train teachers but two schools to train teachers, one at Lexington, the other at Bridgewater. Is that true, Sir?
Mr. Mann.	Quite true, Sir.
Mr. Sumner.	Why — they even tell me that you intend to go to Europe to study educational methods there and to pay for the tour out of your own pocket. Is it true, Sir?
Mr. Mann.	Quite, quite true, Sir.
Mr. Sumner.	And that isn't all I have heard. They tell me that you are going to spend your time running around the country telling people what to teach in the public schools. That can't be true, Sir?
Mr. Mann.	But it is very, very true, Sir.
Mr. Sumner.	I ask you, Dr. Woodward, what manner of man is he? [*Pointing to Mr. Mann*]
Dr. Woodward.	A genius, Mr. Sumner, a genius. I know no other man like him.
Mr. Sumner.	[*Rising and offering his hand*] Mr. Mann, you are a brave gentleman. You have my heartiest best wishes in your new undertaking.
Dr. Woodward.	[*Offering his hand, too*] May God speed you, friend.
Mr. Mann.	Thank you, gentlemen. Henceforward, I shall be no lawyer but a teacher; and education, religious and political freedom will be the watchwords of my life.

[*Music Plays and the Curtain Falls*]

END OF EPISODE III

EPISODE IV
Horace Mann — President of Antioch College

CHARACTERS

HORACE MANN, *President of Antioch College*
and National Educator
MRS. MARY MANN, *his wife*
MR. WILSON, *a political confrere*

AT RISE OF CURTAIN

[*A militant march is played offstage until the curtain has risen. On stage is a simple living-room setting. MRS. MANN and HER HUSBAND are seated in comfortable chairs of the period, he reading, she knitting. The knocker on the door breaks the stillness.*]

MRS. MANN.	How late the hour for one to be calling, Horace!
MR. MANN.	[*Looking at his large vest pocket watch*] Late, indeed, it is, Mary. See who knocks and what help we may give, if help is needed.
MRS. MANN.	[*Dropping her knitting in her work-basket*] You carry the weight of the world on your shoulders, Horace. [*As she proceeds to the door*]
HON. MR. WILSON.	Good evening, Madam. Is Mr. Mann at home?
MRS. MANN.	Why, Mr. Wilson! Of all good people to welcome at this hour of evening! Yes, Mr. Mann is at home here. Do come in and visit with him.
MR. MANN.	[*Rising as the other gentleman enters*] Well — well — well! [*Extending his hand*] I thought the voice was yours, Mr. Wilson. Sit right here and join our happy family.
MR. WILSON.	Then you have not heard the news, Horace?
MR. MANN.	News? NEWS? What news, Sir?
MR. WILSON.	You have been nominated for the governorship of Massachusetts. [*When he seems not to be moved by it*] Sir, have you heard what I just said? I said you have been nominated to the office of Governor of Massachusetts.
MRS. MANN.	Oh, how complimentary, Horace!
MR. WILSON.	I think he does not understand, Madam. Perhaps you . . .

Mr. Mann.	But I do understand, Sir. I have been nominated to the office of Governor of Massachusetts. You do me a great honor, an honor, nevertheless, which I cannot accept.
Mr. Wilson.	You mean, Sir,— you actually mean, Sir, that you decline the nomination?
Mr. Mann.	True, Sir.
Mr. Wilson.	But, Madam, perhaps you . . .
Mrs. Mann.	I could do something with Horace?
Mr. Wilson.	Yes, Madam.
Mrs. Mann.	My husband has already made his own mind up for himself, Mr. Wilson. And I have never known him to decide any really big problem unwisely.
Mr. Mann.	As I said before, friend, the people of Massachusetts do me a great honor. But I have been called to a greater . . .
Mr. Wilson.	Greater, Sir? WE could think of none greater than what we offer you at the moment. You have worked for our children; you have improved our schools; you have established teacher training schools; you have helped every city and town with their special problems; now we ask you to take the problems of the State on your shoulders. To what greater office, could we raise the man who has done so much for us and for our children?
Mr. Mann.	Sir, my work is in education. Today, I have been offered the presidency of Antioch College. I have — well, accepted that offer, Sir.
Mr. Wilson.	Is this true, Madam?
Mrs. Mann.	Very true, Sir.
Mr. Wilson.	[Sadly] The State of Massachusetts has indeed lost a great man.
Mrs. Mann.	True, Sir. But the United States of America, yes, even the world, has found a great EDUCATOR.
Mr. Mann.	I feel very humble. Very humble.
Mr. Wilson.	You need not feel so, Sir. Mrs. Mann is right. The United States of America has found a GREAT EDUCATOR. GOOD LUCK, SIR.

[*Music Plays and Curtain Falls*]

END OF EPISODE IV

EPISODE V
Aftermath — 1937 — The Massachusetts Centennial

CHARACTERS

GOVERNOR OF MASSACHUSETTS
SIX OF HIS GUARDS
NUMBERS OPTIONAL FOR THE FOLLOWING:
    CHILDREN WITH DAISY CHAIN
    REPRESENTATIVE NORMAL SCHOOL STUDENTS
    REPRESENTATIVE NURSES
    REPRESENTATIVE STUDENTS OF ANTIOCH COLLEGE
    REPRESENTATIVE SCHOOL CHILDREN OF AMERICA
    CHILD TO REPRESENT SPIRIT OF EDUCATION
    CHILD TO REPRESENT TYPICAL AMERICAN SCHOOL CHILD

AT RISE OF CURTAIN

[*Set required — an exterior woodland setting, in the center of which is a large monument built in tier fashion. This scene may be a flat backed set or it may be had by getting large trees from woods and banking stage with same for park background. The monument may be made by collecting various sized boxes and placing one on the other until a monument the size required is obtained.*

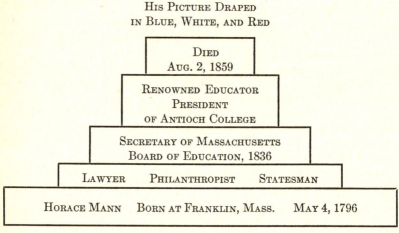

The cartons used to build the above monument could be covered with white crepe paper and inscribed as the one above with suitable letters of construction paper. A large picture of Horace Mann could be placed at the top of the monument and draped in a fitting manner.

At the stage right, a small speaker's stand could be erected and suitably draped for the occasion. White bunting cloth and a blue, white, and red color scheme could be effective.

In the speaker's stand is the Governor of the State of Massachusetts, and to the right and left of the stand are the Governor's staff in full official regalia.

At stage left is a double line of small children (first grade size) carrying a daisy chain. They stand at attention while the Governor speaks. They are dressed in white costumes, and wear a band of daisies in their hair. Off-stage, ready to come on for the GRAND FINALE, and arranged in a double line for orderly procedure for a GRAND MARCH are the following groups:

OFF-STAGE:

a. Twelve or sixteen tall boys and girls from the upper junior high school grades dressed in caps and gowns, and carrying in hands diplomas tied with colorful ribbon. First two carry banner on which is date of the founding by Horace Mann of the first normal school at Lexington, Mass., in 1839. The next two carry banner on which is the date for founding of Bridgewater Normal School.

b. This line of march is followed by a line of girls (upper junior high school size) dressed in nurses' uniforms. Ten or twelve girls would be sufficient with the first two carrying a large banner on which is inscribed the words, WORCESTER HOSPITAL FOR THE INSANE, FOUNDED THROUGH THE EFFORTS OF HORACE MANN IN 1833.

c. Twelve to sixteen more girls and boys dressed in gay sport clothes to represent Antioch College, of which Horace Mann was president from 1852 to 1859. They carry a banner to this effect.

d. Children from all grades dressed in white costumes and carrying American flags come next in line. Of these, there may be any number. The first two carry large banner on which is printed the words, HORACE MANN, FATHER OF COMMON SCHOOL EDUCATION IN MASSACHUSETTS.

e. As a fitting climax, a float made from a child's wagon, and driven by two pages is brought across stage. In the float a small child stands, carrying a torch. She is dressed in the manner of a goddess. From left shoulder to right waist she wears a banner bearing the words, SPIRIT OF AMERICAN EDUCATION. Kneeling at her feet is a smaller child, gazing into her eyes, and holding aloft, so that it is visible to the audience, a huge golden key. On the key may be written the name, HORACE MANN.

As the curtain rises, the GOVERNOR is standing in his box, making the closing speech of the Centennial.]

GOVERNOR. And so, Citizens of this Commonwealth of Massachusetts, such is the story of the life of Horace Mann, Father of Common School Education in our beloved State of Massachusetts. His was a life unparalleled in *devotion to* and *service for* the cause of universal EDUCATION. He was a brilliant lawyer, a humane philanthropist, and a renowned statesman, it is true — but above and beyond all these things, Horace Mann was a GREAT TEACHER. He it was who furnished to us the golden keys of a great democratic system of common school education; to us he handed the torch, to us he gave those keys to preserve undefiled, to cherish untarnished, and to carry unmolested from one generation to the next that the true spirit of a great educational system might not perish from our land. And were Horace Mann here today he would say to you:

> Yon golden keys I give to thee
> To carry on, Massachusetts — TO CARRY ON!

[*Here the band plays a militant martial air, children with daisy chain march around his monument, and the grand march passes across stage as the curtain finally falls.*]

THE END

Mann advocating school improvements before local
Committees throughout the State

HORACE MANN
"FATHER OF FREE PUBLIC SCHOOLS"

A Pageant Depicting Mann's Life at Brown University, His Public Life in Dedham and in the Legislature, Establishment of Board of Education with Horace Mann as Secretary, Establishment of First Public Normal Schools, Mann's Trip to Europe and Criticism of Boston Schools, 1817–1853.

1937

A Pageant

For Junior and Senior High School Presentation

By
Edward S. Murphy
Student, Brockton High School

FATHER OF FREE PUBLIC SCHOOLS

What I can't understand is . . .

HORACE MANN
"FATHER OF FREE PUBLIC SCHOOLS"

SETTINGS

ACT I

Scene 1: Horace Mann's room at Brown University (early summer of 1817).
Scene 2: Library in the home of Dr. Asa Messer (two days later).

ACT II

Scene 1: Home of Atty. Horace Mann in Dedham, Mass. (Summer evening, 1830).
Scene 2: Law office of Horace Mann, Boston (five years later).

ACT III

Scene 1: State Street, Boston (about 1836).
Scene 2: Office of Secretary of Board of Education, Boston (1838).
Scene 3: Home of John Greenleaf Whittier, Cambridge, Mass. (1841).

ACT IV

Scene 1: Convention Hall of Free-Soil Party in Fitchburg, Mass. (1853).

HORACE MANN
"FATHER OF FREE PUBLIC SCHOOLS"

ACT I

CHARACTERS

Horace Mann
John Fisher
William Holmes } *College friends*
Ira Barton
Dr. Asa Messer, *President of Brown University*
Charlotte Messer, *his daughter and Mann's first wife*

Scene 1.

Horace Mann's room at Brown University (early summer of 1817)

[*The room of* Horace Mann *at Brown University, Providence. It is an evening early in the summer of 1817. Seated in a black rocking-chair is* Horace Mann, *a pleasant looking student about twenty years of age. His shoulders are stooped and his head is tipped slightly forward. On a couch are* Ira Barton, *his room-mate, who is short and rather stout, with light hair, and* William Holmes, *a classmate, of medium height and athletic build. Standing in the doorway is* John Fisher, *another classmate, a handsome, dark-haired boy, slightly younger than* Mann.]

FISHER.   What I can't understand is how anyone can shut himself up in a room to study on a warm evening like this.

HOLMES.   Neither can I. And I wouldn't mind if there were any need of it, but you know your marks are the highest in the class, Horace. Why aren't you satisfied?

BARTON.   That's what I tell him. Give some of the rest of us a chance. Why be such a grind? You know, fellows, he spends almost every evening here working away.

FISHER.   It's bad for your health, old man. Why don't you get out in the open and exercise? Even when you do take a little relaxation, what do you do? Play whist!

HOLMES.   No wonder you have the reputation of being the best whist player at Brown.

MANN.   I wish you fellows would leave me alone. What if I do choose
         to make something of my time at college here rather than to
         loaf around half my time like some people I know? I'm sure
         I'd rather be called a grind than a shirker!
BARTON. There you go, Horace, flaring up at the slightest provocation.
         We are thinking only of your good and want you to take it a
         bit easier. I believe I understand what the boys mean.
MANN.   Well, I know I'm fiery and perhaps I am overdoing the studying
         a bit, but you would understand my attitude toward study
         and school better if you knew what I had to contend with during
         my early days. You fellows were different — you had money,
         family and pleasant surroundings. An opportunity to make
         something of my life *means* a lot to me.
FISHER. I suppose that's right. Take me, for instance, I've always had
         the opportunity of enjoying outdoor sports, and I never did
         have to buckle down to hard work.
MANN.   Oh, it isn't work altogether. It is everything connected with my
         life in Franklin, where I was born. My father died when I
         was a youngster, and a year later my brother was drowned
         while swimming. I had to work mighty hard to hold the family
         together. I hardly ever went to school more than eight or ten
         weeks a year until I was about eighteen.
BARTON. Yes, I'd forgotten those things. Don't mind us, Horace. You're
         the best room-mate a fellow ever had. I'm sure if I had been
         forced to put up with what you did, I'd have quit right at the
         beginning.
MANN.   No, you wouldn't, Ira, not if you had met Samuel John Barrett.
FISHER. Samuel John Barrett? Who's he?
MANN.   Barrett was a teacher who came to Franklin about two years
         ago. He was a peculiar character — a genius when it came to
         the classics, but he knew scarcely nothing about mathematics.
         It was he who gave me my first insight into literature. It was
         under his tutoring that I prepared for college and was able
         to enter the sophomore class here at Brown.
HOLMES. He must have been a remarkable character.
MANN.   He was. Why, he could hear a lesson in the "Aeneid" or "Cicero"
         and never take a grammar or text book in his hands. I re-
         member I offended him one day by handing him my book when
         he was going to set the next lesson.
BARTON. How long did it take you to prepare for college?
MANN.   Thanks to Barrett, only a little over six months. He gave me the
         determination to let nothing stand in my way of getting an
         education, and I intend to succeed no matter what it costs me
         in the way of effort. I hope I live to see the day when our

schools are presided over by teachers like Samuel John Barrett rather than by the unskilled, ignorant instructors such as have charge of our rural schools today.

FISHER.   I only wish I had your grit and energy. Didn't I hear you say you intend to enter Litchfield Law School after you graduate from Brown?

MANN.   Yes, that is my greatest desire; and if I ever do become a lawyer, it won't be as an unscrupulous defender of criminals. Such a lawyer is the greatest criminal of all. His is the evil spirit that conspires with the criminal to do evil and yet escape punishment.

HOLMES.   You'll never make any money that way.

MANN.   No, perhaps I won't get rich, but I'll have the satisfaction of knowing that I am fighting for the truth. I believe that the conscious conviction of being right renders its possessor more than a match for his antagonist, otherwise his superior.

BARTON.   I never thought about it that way, but there is a great deal in what you say. By the way, Fisher, what do you propose to do?

FISHER.   Oh, I plan to enter a theological school. My father is a minister, you know. He's always planned to have me follow in his footsteps and I feel he's right about it.

HOLMES.   My, but we're getting serious tonight. We came up here to coax Horace from his books and instead we've settled down for an evening's discussion.

BARTON.   Well, let's change the subject. What's this I hear about the plan of the boys to break into the chapel and hold the Fourth of July celebration there?

FISHER.   It's all fixed. Tomorrow night the three upper classes meet. We want to make this a real celebration. So, in spite of President Messer's "No", we are going to go right through with our plans and break into the chapel. What a lark we'll have!

HOLMES.   Say, Mann, you're to give the Fourth of July oration. How about giving it in the chapel tomorrow night?

BARTON.   That's an original plan. What do you say to that, Horace?

MANN.   Breaking into the chapel seems like rather overdoing the celebration. But I do think that President Messer is wrong in depriving us of the use of the chapel; yet, he'd be greatly offended if we went directly against his wishes!

FISHER.   Is it President Messer that you do not wish to offend or his charming daughter, Charlotte? Seems to me I've heard she thinks rather well of our leading student, and perhaps he doesn't want to lower himself in her estimation.

MANN.   Charlotte Messer? Why, she wouldn't even look at a country bumpkin like me. I'm sure she admires the athletic type. Besides, what I do is never influenced by the opinion someone may have of me —

BARTON.   There you go again, Horace, getting angry without reason. What we want is that oration in the chapel. It is just the touch to make our celebration complete.

HOLMES.   Come on, Horace! I dare you to come along and make the speech.

MANN.   Well, I think we are carrying things a trifle too far, but I'm with you and my speech will be heard in the chapel tomorrow night.

FISHER.   Good for you, Horace!

HOLMES.   Now our celebration will be something to remember.

BARTON.   Come on! Let's all take a walk down College Hill and talk over our plans.

CURTAIN

SCENE 2.

Library in the home of Dr. Asa Messer (two days later)

[*The library in the home of Dr. Asa Messer, President of Brown University, two days later. DR. MESSER is seated at his desk and before him stands HORACE MANN.*]

DR. MESSER. Well, Mann, to express myself mildly, may I say that I am dumfounded that one of your scholastic standing should take part in such an affair as occurred last night?

MANN.   Yes, Sir, I suppose you are surprised.

DR. MESSER. That's it — surprised. I rather thought you were a quiet, studious young man. Whatever possessed you to be a party to this escapade?

MANN.   Dr. Messer, when I feel an injustice is being done, I can never stand idly by. I considered it an injustice to deprive the students of the use of the chapel for their celebration, and under the circumstances, I ask that in fairness you overlook the affair.

DR. MESSER. Overlook the breaking of my commands? Overlook the shooting of fireworks from the Memorial Tower? Why, I find it difficult to refrain from expelling you all! Who were the leaders in this celebration?

MANN.   I'd rather not say, Sir.

[*The door opens slowly and CHARLOTTE MESSER enters her father's study. She is slight in build, an extremely attractive girl of about seventeen or eighteen. She has small features and large dark eyes. She glances at Horace and then advances toward her father's desk.*]

CHARLOTTE.	Oh, father, I was just passing through the hall and couldn't help hearing what you were saying. Really, I wasn't eavesdropping. I know Mr. Mann wasn't to blame, even though he won't say so. Father, it *was* Fourth of July you know, and I'm sure Horace — I mean Mr. Mann — made a perfectly eloquent speech, even if it was delivered in the Memorial Chapel.
DR. MESSER.	That will be enough, Charlotte, and if you will please step outside into the hall, being certain to close the door firmly after you, I feel that I can handle the situation satisfactorily.
CHARLOTTE.	Yes, father.

[Exit Charlotte]

DR. MESSER.	It seems you have an advocate at court, Mann.
MANN.	Well, Sir, if you'll permit me, I'm perfectly willing to take my punishment for the affair in the chapel. Miss Messer is very kind, but I don't believe she understands about the fireworks.
DR. MESSER.	However, I believe I understand, and I intend to make your punishment fit the crime.
MANN.	Yes, Sir.
DR. MESSER.	I'm going to fine you the sum of one dollar to be donated to the hospital fund of the college.
MANN.	Thank you, Dr. Messer.
DR. MESSER.	Very well, lad. By the way, I understand that you intend to study law at Litchfield.
MANN.	Yes, Sir, I hope to.
DR. MESSER.	When you're practicing law, Mann, remember your experience this morning and profit by it. A lawyer's most successful plea is made when his heart is in his client's case.
MANN.	I'll remember, Dr. Messer.
DR. MESSER.	And I wouldn't be surprised in this instance if the lawyer were waiting for the client just outside that door.

CURTAIN

ACT II

CHARACTERS

Horace Mann
Dr. Asa Messer, *President of Brown University*
Charlotte Messer, *his daughter and Mann's first wife*

Scene 1.

The living room of the home of Attorney Horace Mann in Dedham, Massachusetts.

[*It is a summer evening thirteen years later. Mann is now a member of the Massachusetts State Legislature and a leading citizen of the town. Horace, aged about thirty-three, is seated at a table writing, while his wife sits before the fireplace busily sewing. He raises his head and speaks.*]

Mann.	Did I tell you, Charlotte, what they've asked me to do? Act as orator on Fourth of July. Seems to me that the citizens of Dedham have heard enough of me.
Charlotte.	Nonsense, Horace, as if anyone could ever hear too many of your eloquent words. How they applaud you, and how I love to listen to their cheers.
Mann.	I forget the applause of the world for your more precious congratulations and approving voice. There are those who do not acclaim me.
Charlotte.	Do they matter?
Mann.	Not to me perhaps, but I burn with indignation when I consider how they are combating the finest things that have ever come to this town. Take the temperance society, for instance; because as its president I broke up the habit of "treating" the electors after the election was over, I have been the victim of the most unfair criticism.
Charlotte.	I know; and then for charitable purposes you gave away an even greater sum than the "treating" would have cost.
Mann.	They charge that my conduct sprang from unworthy motives. Why, even today one of the opposition declared he was coming to the house here this very night to question me. I'll tell him! I'll give him such a verbal lashing that he'll never forget it. I stand for what is right, and no one can impugn my motives.
Charlotte.	Calm yourself, dear Horace. Do not permit your anger to overcome your kindly manner and pleasant ways.
Mann.	Forgive me, Charlotte, but I have no patience with men who seek to corrupt the habits of our town and who interfere with what does not concern them.

CHARLOTTE.	Do you remember a Fourth of July oration you made many years ago in Memorial Chapel at Brown?
MANN.	Shall I ever forget it, or your father's anger? If it hadn't been for you, perhaps I would have been expelled.
CHARLOTTE.	Did you think I was bold to interfere with my father's affairs.
MANN.	Bold? Never! I thought you were most gracious and kind.
CHARLOTTE.	Sometimes I wonder if all who interfere in other people's affairs aren't doing it to be kind, in your opinion.
MANN.	What a perfect help-mate you are! Your grace and charm have made our home the social center of Dedham. You have brought me happiness such as I have never known.
CHARLOTTE.	And I am happy, too. The wife of Dedham's leading citizen, surrounded by kind friends and acquaintances. If my strength but equalled yours, how it would please me to assist you in the great civic work you are doing. If only I were stronger and did not get so weary!
MANN.	Your counsel and kindness are worth everything to me.
CHARLOTTE.	Will you promise, Horace, that when that visitor comes to-night, you will not allow yourself to lose your temper no matter what he says?
MANN.	I'll promise, Charlotte, dear. There'll never be an unkind word spoken. [*Continues with his writing.*]

[*A knock is heard at the door.*]

CURTAIN

SCENE 2.

Law Office of Horace Mann

[*The law office of* HORACE MANN *in Boston, Massachusetts, about five years later.* HORACE MANN *is seated at his desk and in a chair beside him is* DR. ASA MESSER, *now an elderly man.*]

DR. MESSER.	My dear son, Charlotte's death makes you all the more dear to us. We are worried about you. I pray you, dear Horace, take care of your health. We fear you are working too hard as a member of the State Legislature.
MANN.	I understand, Dr. Messer, but when engrossed in business my thoughts steal away to Charlotte. Every pleasure I ever knew was instantly doubled by the thought that I would repeat it to her.

DR. MESSER.   Take to your heart the consolation that dear Charlotte has left you, and have courage for her sake.

MANN.   It is the memory of her love and loyalty that have given me the courage and inspiration to fight against the narrow prejudices that face me in the Legislature.

DR. MESSER.   Your first speech on religious liberty attracted wide attention. The Providence newspaper printed the complete story of your great victory.

MANN.   It is discouraging sometimes to realize that my fellow-legislators are so reactionary. They declare that railroads will ruin the small towns. Instead, railroads have constituted one of the great civilizing agencies in every community. I declare that railroads increase the cost of living in a community, but they multiply the resources from which that additional cost is to be met.

DR. MESSER.   I am certain, Horace, that with your determination and eloquence, you will persuade the Legislature to follow your views.

MANN.   My greatest work is before me, Dr. Messer. Tomorrow I am determined to advocate the establishment of a State insane hospital at Worcester.

DR. MESSER.   A splendid project.

MANN.   My foes characterize it as a project of boyish enthusiasm. How can anyone be opposed to such a great humanitarian plan?

DR. MESSER.   The expense will be great.

MANN.   More than $180,000 a year. But consider the poor victims of insanity and how badly they are being treated now. While the Legislature delays, they suffer. Can any cost be too great to restore these unfortunates to health?

DR. MESSER.   I know you will succeed, Horace, because you are in the right, and right must prevail.

MANN.   Thank you, Dr. Messer, you are a kind friend and adviser.

DR. MESSER.   Good-bye, Horace, and God prosper you.

CURTAIN

ACT III

CHARACTERS

JOHN FISHER } *Friends of Horace Mann*
IRA BARTON }

HORACE MANN

JOHN G. CARTER, *Advocate of the Massachusetts Board of Education*

CYRUS PEIRCE, *Principal of Lexington Normal School*

MARY PEABODY MANN, *Mann's second wife*

JOHN GREENLEAF WHITTIER } *Friends of Horace Mann*
CHARLES SUMNER }

SCENE 1.

State Street in Boston.

[*The year is 1836.* JOHN FISHER, *dressed in clerical garb, is standing on a corner when he is approached by* IRA BARTON, *who has just alighted from a carriage nearby.*]

BARTON. I'm pleased to meet the Reverend Mr. Fisher whose influential sermons are so widely read.

FISHER. You flatter me, Doctor Barton, but I'm glad to see you again. You don't mention your medical discoveries and how noted you have become. I read only this morning that you have given a series of lectures at Harvard University.

BARTON. I suppose we both have succeeded more than we deserve. By the way, did you hear about the death of Dr. Messer of Brown?

FISHER. Yes, it was very sad. His daughter's death was a great blow to him and to our old friend, Horace Mann, as well. Do you remember when we were all at Brown together and how hard Horace studied and how he planned to become a great lawyer?

BARTON. Senator Horace Mann! It seems hardly possible! I was in the gallery of the House the day he made his wonderful address in favor of the Worcester asylum. I saw an editorial which said, "We have not heard a speech during the session which seemed to occupy more of the undivided attention of the House than Mr. Mann's."

FISHER. He certainly had the satisfaction of seeing the enactment of a measure which placed thirty thousand dollars at the service of a commission to establish a hospital at Worcester. I understand he has been made chairman of the commission.

BARTON. Have you read about the great effort he is making to establish a Board of Education? I, for one, hope he will succeed.

FISHER. So do I! Even though some of my fellow-ministers are opposed to the measure. If they knew Horace Mann as I do, they would know that anything he advocated or supported was above reproach.

BARTON.   You are not alone in that belief. See how he is returned to office
again and again with increasing majorities.

FISHER.   Well, I'm sorry, Ira, but I have an appointment. I must be
leaving.

BARTON.   Good-bye, John. When you are in Lowell, be sure to pay me a
visit.

FISHER.   Thank you. I shall be pleased to do so. Good-bye.

CURTAIN

SCENE 2.

The office of Horace Mann, Secretary of the Board of Education, in
Boston.

[*The year is 1838.* HORACE MANN *is seated at his desk and beside him is*
JOHN G. CARTER, *a middle-aged gentleman with gray beard and gray hair.*]

CARTER.   But, Governor Everett insisted that you become Secretary of the
Board of Education. We need a great statesman and educator
such as you.

MANN.   No, Mr. Carter, I felt by every consideration that you should have
been secretary. You have worked steadily for the improvement
of our educational system in every manner.

CARTER.   I am too deeply interested in the success of the Board to have
wanted anyone but you to serve as its secretary. I thank you
for acceding to the wishes of the Governor.

MANN.   I wonder if I can adequately perform the duties! In undertaking
this task I must encounter privation, labor and infinite annoy-
ance from an infinite number of schemers. I must condense the
steam of enthusiasm and soften the rock of the incredulous.
What toil in arriving at a true school system! What toil in
infusing that system into the minds of others!

CARTER.   We all feel there is no individual in the Commonwealth of Massachusetts better suited to this great task than you. Perhaps the
salary may not be great, but think of the honor of the position.

MANN.   Salary! Don't speak to me of salary or honor of position, Mr.
Carter. My only thought in accepting was of the service I might
render.

CARTER.   I knew, Mr. Mann, that you were almost certain to be chosen
President of the Senate, and, of course, there is more dignity
and honor in being at the head of that great body.

MANN.   Mr. Carter, you may tell Governor Everett that I am happy at
                having accepted the position of Secretary of the Board of Educa-
                tion. If the Lord will prosper me for ten years, I will show every-
                one what way the balance of honor lies between being President
                of the Senate and Secretary of the Board of Education.
CARTER.   May success attend your efforts. Good-bye, Mr. Mann.
MANN.   Good-bye, Mr. Carter.

[Exit Mr. Carter.]

*[As Mr. Carter leaves, CYRUS PEIRCE, a distinguished looking gentleman with
iron gray hair, enters.]*

MANN.   Good afternoon, Mr. Peirce, won't you be seated? I've called you
                here for a very important reason. The Board of Education has
                decided to establish two normal schools, one at Lexington for
                young ladies and one at Barre for both sexes. I want you to take
                charge of the school at Lexington.
PEIRCE.   I appreciate the honor you bestow upon me by offering me this
                position, but I am happily situated in Nantucket. My home
                and family are there. Furthermore, I feel you are more capable
                than I.
MANN.   This normal school is my idea. I have given it a great deal of
                thought and I have considered all the desirable persons suitable
                to act as principal of such a school. Mr. Peirce, I know of no
                one as well adapted to the place as you, and I feel it your duty
                to the State and to the young people to accept the position.
PEIRCE.   Mr. Mann, I have always admired your work from the beginning,
                and, under the circumstances, I am glad to have a part in this
                great enterprise so fraught with large possibilities. In accepting
                this appointment, let me say that I would rather die than fail
                in this undertaking.
MANN.   Thank you, Mr. Peirce. I feel as you do, that "study enough will
                make a pupil master of anything he is capable of learning," and
                your teaching will inspire a love of learning for its own sake.

*[There is a gentle rap at the door. Mann arises and admits MARY PEABODY
MANN, a dignified lady of about average height. She is extremely aristocratic in
appearance.]*

MANN.   How do you do, my dear Mary? It is indeed a pleasure to welcome
                you. Permit me to introduce Mr. Cyrus Peirce of Nantucket,
                who has just done me the honor of accepting the principalship
                of the first normal school. My wife — Mary Peabody Mann.
MARY.   How do you do, Mr. Peirce? I have heard Mr. Mann speak of you
                so often and I knew of his anxiety to have you become the head
                of his new school.
PEIRCE.   It is indeed a pleasure to greet you, Mrs. Mann.

MANN.   I have no doubt Mr. Peirce is acquainted with your brother-in-law, Mary, Mr. Nathaniel Hawthorne.

PEIRCE.   Yes, indeed. We have spent many hours together in Cambridge and he has promised to visit me at Nantucket. Perhaps you will both join him and make a trip to our lovely island.

MARY.   Thank you.

MANN.   And you must visit us, Mr. Peirce, in our new home in West Newton just as soon as we return from Europe.

PEIRCE.   Thank you, Mr. Mann. I shall be pleased to accept your invitation. How long do you intend to remain abroad? Do you intend to visit many countries?

MANN.   Oh, several months. It is my good fortune to have received invitations from the educators of the leading countries of the old world, and they have promised to permit me to study their educational systems.

PEIRCE.   You certainly deserve a vacation if anyone ever did and I hope you enjoy a most entertaining and instructive journey to England and the continent. Now I must bid you and Mrs. Mann good-day.

MANN.   Good-bye, Mr. Peirce. Tomorrow we shall talk at greater length upon our plans for the new normal school.

MARY.   Good-bye, Mr. Peirce.

[*Exit Mr. Peirce.*]

MARY.   Europe! It seems hard to believe that at last you have consented to take time enough to enjoy a well-earned rest. What a mental stimulation you will gain from being able to observe foreign systems of education in actual operation!

MANN.   And what material I shall gather from abroad for my next report for the Board of Education! Can you picture the indignation of my enemies and critics when they read my comparisons of our educational system with those in vogue abroad?

MARY.   What toil and sacrifice you have put into your work! How conscientiously you have given your devotion to the advancement of education in Massachusetts! I do wish you would learn to spare yourself. Remember, Horace, your life is not only precious to the Commonwealth, but even more so to me.

MANN.   Thanks to your love and inspiration, I have been given the strength to fight on, and will continue to do so until I have achieved my ideals for the promotion of the general welfare.

MARY.   Come, Horace, let us depart. The carriage is waiting at the door.

CURTAIN

SCENE 3.

The living room of the home of John Greenleaf Whittier,
Cambridge, Mass.

[*The year is 1841. Seated are* JOHN GREENLEAF WHITTIER *and* CHARLES
SUMNER.]

WHITTIER.   I consider it an outrage that Secretary Mann should have been
permitted to pay his own expenses of his trip to Europe. Seems
to me that the State of Massachusetts should have been
willing to defray every penny of the cost.

SUMNER.   No one ever worked harder for the people of Massachusetts than
Mr. Mann, and I hear words of indignation from all sides that
he should have been forced to foot the cost of the journey.

WHITTIER.   I feel certain that within a few months something will be done
about the matter. But Horace is proud, you know, and may
refuse to accept anything from the State.

SUMNER.   By the way, have you read his latest report? It has certainly
stirred up the Masters' Association of Boston. Listen to this:
"While in Saxony I never saw a teacher hear a lesson with a
book in hand, and never saw a child arraigned for punishment,
under-going it, or having been recently punished." Then he
goes on to compare certain conditions in the local schools most
unfavorably with those he visited abroad.

WHITTIER.   I'm afraid our good friend, Horace, has stirred up a hornets'
nest. I understand that the Masters' Association is preparing
to attack his ideas and are going to visit various cities in an
effort to discredit him.

SUMNER.   Have you seen their pamphlet referring to Horace Mann's
Report?

WHITTIER.   Yes, I read it, and Mann's answer also. It would appear to me
that Horace was in a perfect rage when he wrote his "Reply".
But then, one can hardly blame him when one considers the
difficulties with which he has had to contend.

SUMNER.   That's right. How hard he worked on his normal school program! Think of it! He practically forced the Legislature to
appropriate the ten thousand dollars to finance the two schools
he opened, one in Lexington and the other in Barre. Then he
secured Mr. Peirce, a most worthy teacher.

WHITTIER.   Then only three young lady pupils appeared when the school
opened; but they tell me Mr. Peirce continued with the work
and this past year a class of forty-two was graduated.

SUMNER.   I believe that Horace Mann will succeed with his normal school
plan and that he will win a complete victory for the cause of
education that will advance the schools of this Commonwealth

to unusual and wonderful heights. However, Mann is facing a crisis at the present time. I am afraid the public is beginning to lose confidence in him.

WHITTIER.   Is there some manner in which we can assist him?

SUMNER.   John, I believe I have a solution. Why not secure the aid of our mutual friends, Josiah Quincy, Edward Everett, Henry Wilson and Theodore Parker? Let us solicit among the bankers and professional men the sum of five thousand dollars and we will ask the legislature for a like sum. This money will be placed in the hands of the Board of Education for the improvement of schools, and in this way we shall indicate our confidence in Horace Mann and his work.

WHITTIER.   A splendid idea! With well-known men giving Horace Mann their support, public confidence will return and he will be victor in this great conflict.

CURTAIN

ACT IV

CHARACTERS

JOHN FISHER⎫ *Friends of Horace Mann*
IRA BARTON ⎭
CHAIRMAN OF THE CONVENTION
HORACE MANN

SCENE 1.

The Convention Hall of the Free-Soil Party in Fitchburg, Massachusetts.
[*It is late afternoon, September 19, 1853. The scene is the stage on which are representative citizens and delegates. At the extreme left are seated* REVEREND JOHN FISHER *and* DR. IRA BARTON.]

BARTON.   What a stirring scene and how fortunate to have you as my guest on this unusual occasion!

FISHER.   It is a great satisfaction for me to attend my first political convention and to have the opportunity of once more seeing our friend and schoolmate, Horace Mann.

BARTON.   He has led a remarkable life and has risen to great heights. To think that the frail-appearing Horace Mann of our school days would live to take the place of the great John Quincy Adams in the United States Congress.

FISHER.   What a sterling fighter for the cause of slavery Mann was! And how he fought against the compromising attitude of Daniel Webster!

BARTON.   Will you ever forget the Drayton case and how heroically he defended the captain and his crew in that famous trial amid such hostile surroundings?

FISHER.   I always felt that decision was unfair, particularly after the great plea advanced by Mann.

BARTON.   I believe that Horace is weary of politics. Think of anyone having the opportunity of being Governor of this Commonwealth and giving up the chance. He has been an outstanding figure in this State and it is a great loss to the people of Massachusetts to have him depart.

FISHER.   He is on his way to Ohio now, is he not, to take up his duties at Antioch College?

BARTON.   Yes, he has finally accepted the presidency of that institution. Once more he is going to take up the work of education and in an entirely new field.

FISHER.   Listen! What is that?

[*A band is heard approaching outside. The music is mingled with distant shouts and cheers.*]

BARTON.   Here he comes now! How proud he looks!

[*Horace Mann, now an elderly gentleman, enters from the right, accompanied by a group of delegates, and advances to the center of the stage amid tremendous applause from the audience. The chairman of this convention arises and shakes hands with Mann and then raps for order.*]

CHAIRMAN.   When your committee learned that the train bearing the former leader of our Free-Soil Party was to pass through this city on the way to Yellow Springs, Ohio, we deemed it a great privilege to appoint a delegation to go to the railroad station to greet him.   At great inconvenience to himself, he has consented to take passage on a later train, and it becomes my pleasure to present to you that great educator, patriot and reformer, the president of Antioch College, the Honorable Horace Mann.

[*Cheers and applause*]

MANN.   Mr. Chairman, invited guests, and delegates to this great Free-Soil Convention: May I thank you heartily for the distinguished honor you have conferred upon me?   It is my pleasant hope that the party may meet in the future the success it so richly deserves.   I feel that it is a time to speak from the heart, for I am going out to a new field to labor under new conditions, leaving the friends of my youth, manhood and middle life.   Were I entitled to speak in the character of a patriot and of a stateman, I would say first and chiefest, maintain these three great measures, or I might call them great institutions — temperance, education and freedom.   Were I entitled as a Christian or a man of piety to utter my supplication before you on this occasion, as such a Christian and as such a man of piety, I should say, strive first of all for the three great blessings, the greatest blessings ever enjoyed on earth — temperance, education, and freedom.   It rejoices me to think, in giving you a sad, though kind farewell, that the three last words I shall perhaps ever utter before a Massachusetts audience are the three words — TEMPERANCE, EDUCATION AND FREEDOM.

[*Applause*]

CURTAIN

Mr. and Mrs. Mann on their European tour
"The sight of one child educated to understand something of his Maker,
and of that Maker's work, is a far more glorious spectacle than all
the cathedrals which the art of man has ever reared."

THE GREAT CRUSADER

Horace Mann in Symbolic Pageantry

1937

A Pageant

For Presentation by Senior High Schools,
Teachers Colleges, and Citizen Groups

By
Emily T. Thompson, A. B.,
Holyoke, Massachusetts

THE GREAT CRUSADER

In our country . . .

"In our country, and in our times, no man is worthy the honored name of a statesman, who does not include the highest practicable education of the people in all his plans of administration. He may have eloquence, he may have a knowledge of all history, diplomacy, jurisprudence; and by these he might claim, in other countries, the elevated rank of a statesman; but, unless he speaks, plans, labors, at all times and in all places, for the culture and edification of the whole people, he is not, he cannot be, an American statesman."

— *Horace Mann.*

THE GREAT CRUSADER

EPISODES

Prologue

Episode I: Vision of Horace Mann

Episode II: A Dream Come True

Episode III: The Recall to the Cause of Education

THE GREAT CRUSADER

Prologue

CHARACTERS

DEMOCRACY
EDUCATION
PURITAN
YOUTH
CHORUS

Scene

[*Any draped or simple background with a back drop on which could be thrown the outlines of the cutout. At the back of the stage an elevation of four or five steps on which the symbolic figures may be posed. The cutout on the screen shows the Temple of Learning, to which there are steps leading.*

THE PURITAN *is standing on the right of the centre of the stage. A little above him and to the left stands a* YOUTH *of the same period. At the foot of the stairs, on the left,* DEMOCRACY *stands; and on the third step, right center,* EDUCATION *stands.*]

PURITAN.   The mighty ocean with sonorous beatings against the rock-strewn coasts of a virgin land strikes out a new song, a song of strength wherein lies hope for every man.

Through high arched forests, cool and fragrant, the song reverberates until the echoes from a thousand aisles roll into an anthem grand, that sounds against the age-old hills and rebounds back again, a challenge for every man.

Hope, challenge and the faith of God — these treasures do ye offer, O Democracy, to those that have the strength to make that hope a reality, that challenge an undying goal, and that faith a bulwark against the foes of man.

YOUTH.   Vanguard of a great crusade we stand, in which we dedicate our lives to human rights. Upon this jousting field the sword of hate will break. Freedom will be the quest — freedom to worship God — freedom to develop the deep resources of the mind. The favor of Democracy and of her handmaiden we will bind upon our sleeves.

DEMOCRACY. See beyond the distant plain, where the too eager evening sky is dimmed by evening dews, the hope of heaven streams out in myriad colors like rainbow strands that promise fulfillment of all the endeavors of a new day. The dawn of that day appears beyond the gray horizon. My sons will seek the truth.

Swing wide the gates of the Castle of Learning. Forevermore may they be open to all who seek to enter in. Throughout the ages a great cavalcade will move, ever adding strength to strength. O Youth, the voice of a new day, send out the challenge to all men of all classes, of all creeds, to make themselves worthy of their great heritage.

CHORUS. O beautiful for patriot dream
     That sees beyond the years,
Thine alabaster cities gleam
     Undimm'd by human tears.
America! America!
     God shed His grace on thee,
And crown thy good with brotherhood
     From sea to shining sea!

INTERLUDE: *Interpretative Dance* — SOWING AND HARVEST.
     Tchaikowsky arranged by Chalif.

TABLEAU

YOUTH *ascends the stairs between* DEMOCRACY *and* EDUCATION. *He receives the shield and the lights dim out after a minute.*

INTERLUDE: *Interpretative Music (short period).*

[*The author suggests a rhythmic interpretation of the forces of battle in which Freedom is victorious, but then the shadows of the aftermath of war darken the scene.*]

SPEECH CHOIR. The cavalcade moves on. Now Tyranny stalks abroad throughout the land and war sounds its battlecry to save the new Democracy. The din of war is hushed, but the dark veil of poverty and selfishness dim the brightness of the new world. Slowly the gates to the Castle of Learning are closed.

EPISODE I
Vision of Horace Mann

CHARACTERS

DEMOCRACY
EDUCATION
YOUTH
SECOND YOUTH
CHORUS
SEVEN DEADLY SINS
AGED KEEPER
THE CRUSADER

SCENE 1.
The Consecration

[Sinister shadows dim the outlines of the Castle of Learning. A YOUTH of another generation stands before the gates, pleading for entrance. EDUCATION stands within the gates unable to open them.]

DEMOCRACY.   Too many of my sons knock in vain at your gates, O Education. What evil is this that has come upon your ways? Have you forgotten the heritage of the past, the promise of a new world? What thwarts the crusade for free schools and a free people?

EDUCATION.   Not mine alone is the fault with which you upbraid me. No longer is equal opportunity the law of the land. Wealth holds the keys to the Castle of Learning. Under the cruel lash of labor, the shoulders of your children bend. The light of hope has died within their eyes.

DEMOCRACY.   Despair not, for many voices are being lifted up to right this wrong. The great crusade will once again find a champion for its cause.

EDUCATION.   Yet only a great crusader can put to rout the foes of education. He must know the longings and the pain of thwarted hopes. Within his heart must dwell the love for all humanity; and he must have vision and the courage sustained by unfaltering faith.

2ND YOUTH.   O Democracy, I fain would wear your favor on my sleeve as did the knights of old. Within the courts of Ignorance and Selfishness I would throw down your gage for the cause of my fellow men. Full trained am I, for I have toiled upon the hungry land; but in the flickering candle light at my mother's knee I learned to reverence the

	ideals of education. Gird me with the sword of Faith and put on my arm the shield of Truth and with the Love of all mankind within my heart I will wage battle till the gates of Education swing wide forevermore.
EDUCATION.	What Oath will you subscribe to that will prove you worthy of this high endeavor?
2ND YOUTH.	I believe in the existence of a great immortal, immutable principle of natural law or natural ethics — a principle of divine origin — which proves the absolute right to an education of every human being that comes into the world.
	How shall our love of country, if any, be made manifest? How, but by laboring for our descendants — not in the same way, but with the same fidelity — as our fathers labored for us.
DEMOCRACY.	Bind upon your arm the shield of Truth and gird yourself with the sword of Faith. Again a great crusader goes forth to battle for the ideals of Democracy.

[*The Youth binds upon his arm the shield of Truth. He kneels before* DEMOCRACY *who dubs him her Knight. Then he receives from her the sword of Faith.*]

| CHORUS. | *Onward Christian Soldiers, etc.* |

SCENE 2.

The Quest

[*The scene darkens. Before the gates of the Castle of Learning the* SEVEN DEADLY SINS, *clad in dull gray armor, guard the entrance. The* SINS *are:* IGNORANCE, INTOLERANCE, SELFISHNESS, WEALTH, GREED, INDIFFERENCE, *and* PREJUDICE. *An* AGED KEEPER *stands, left center.*]

THE CRUSADER.	Aged Keeper of the Gate, Give me the Keys to the Castle.
KEEPER.	That I may not, for the foes of Education guard the approaches to the Castle.
THE CRUSADER.	Then I will challenge them to combat. The sword of Faith will be their undoing.
KEEPER.	That were too unequal a task for any one knight.
THE CRUSADER.	The love of all humanity which dwells within my heart will give me strength. No man can defy the power of love. Ye Deadly Sins, disperse, that the gates of the Castle may swing wide for all men.

IGNORANCE. It is well that all should enter here. Unsheath your sword and we will do battle with you.

THE CRUSADER. Will ye all have at me at once?

INTOLERANCE. That we will and at once.

THE CRUSADER. Mark well the power of Truth and the sword of Faith. All the powers of evil can not dismay me or overcome the right.

[*The scene is symbolic representation of struggle between Good and Evil and ends with the tableau showing the Knight victorious.*]

[*During all this time the Chorus has been singing in the distance "Onward Christian Soldiers".*]

[*The lights dim and the Sins exeunt.*]

TABLEAU

THE CRUSADER *receives the keys from the* KEEPER *and swings wide the gates.* EDUCATION *receives the* CRUSADER, *and the* HANDMAIDENS OF EDUCATION *give an interpretative dance of Victory.*

EPISODE II
A Dream Come True

CHARACTERS

JAMES G. CARTER
EMERSON DAVIS
EDMUND DWIGHT
HORACE MANN
EDWARD NEWTON
ROBERT RANTOUL, JR.
THOMAS ROBBINS
JARED SPARKS

These men composed the first Board of Education in Massachusetts in 1837.

DEMOCRACY
EDUCATION
THE CRUSADER (KNIGHT)
CHORUS
MRS. CYRUS PEIRCE
CYNTHIA SMITH
DOROTHY ADAMS, *a school teacher*
SEVERAL OTHER GUESTS
MARTHA, *a maid*
GROUP OF TEACHERS
GROUP OF STUDENTS
HON. BARKER BURNELL

SCENE 1.

[*In the background is a tableau of* DEMOCRACY *and* EDUCATION *placing a victory crown on the* KNIGHT. *In the foreground* THE EIGHT MEN *are grouped about a table.*]

DWIGHT.   Gentlemen, a great opportunity lies before us and with that opportunity there devolves upon us a grave responsibility. This Board of Education, appointed by the Governor of this great Commonwealth is the vanguard of a great crusade. What is our first duty, then?

MANN.   Our first duty is the establishment of free schools for all our children. If we do not prepare our children to become good citizens, if we do not develop their capacities, if we do not enrich their minds with knowledge, imbue their hearts with the love of truth and beauty and a reverence for all things sacred and holy, then our republic must go down to destruction as others have gone before it.

NEWTON.	That is the first duty to our fellow citizens, but our esteemed friend, Mr. Dwight, has said that this movement is the beginning of a great crusade. We have a great cause, but we need as Secretary of this Board a Great Crusader.
DWIGHT.	There is no one who has the cause of humanity closer to his heart, no one who has greater eloquence to stir the indifferent minds of our fellow citizens than our colleague, Horace Mann. Honored Sir, we know that you have thought this matter over prayerfully. We appreciate the sacrifice that the acceptance of this post will entail. The cause is worthy. It needs a worthy leader. Sir, what is your decision?
MANN.	I have today sent to the Governor of the Commonwealth this letter from which I will read: "Henceforth, so long as I hold this office I devote myself to the supremest welfare of mankind on earth. An inconceivably greater labor is undertaken. With the highest degree of prosperity, results will manifest themselves but slowly. The harvest is far distant from the seedtime. Faith is the only sustainer. I have faith in the improvability of the race — in their accelerating improvability. This effort may do, apparently, but little. But a mere beginning a good cause is never little. Men can resist the influence of talent; they will deny demonstration, if need be; but few will combat goodness for any length of time. Love is a universal solvent. Here is a clew given by God to lead us through the labyrinth of the world."

[*The lights down stage are dimmed, but the light is brought up in the back where* DEMOCRACY *stands alone, holding the shield and with torch uplifted in her right hand.*]

CHORUS.	*Land of Hope and Glory. Elgar.*

SCENE 2.
The Home of Cyrus Peirce in Nantucket.

[MRS. CYRUS PEIRCE, CYNTHIA SMITH, DOROTHY ADAMS, a school teacher, and some other guests. *They are all dressed attractively in the costume of 1837. The scene is the parlor in the Peirce Home. As the lights go up, a group of half-dozen or more ladies are talking with each other in excited tones. There is a knock at the door and the maid ushers in* Cynthia Smith. Mrs. Peirce *goes to greet her.*]

Mrs. Peirce.	Do come in, Cynthia. Martha will take your bonnet and shawl.
Cynthia.	Have your guests arrived, my dear? I am so anxious to meet Horace Mann. You know my friends say he is like one inspired. Some one has called him "The Great Crusader."
Mrs. Peirce.	He is a great crusader and yet withal he is a very gentle knight who believes in the efficacy of love. He says, "A spirit mildly devoting itself to a good cause is a certain conqueror".
Dorothy Adams.	[*Joining Mrs. Peirce and Cynthia*] I overheard you quoting one of Horace Mann's sayings. In the educational field he is the topic of the day. No teacher in Massachusetts could fail to be inspired by his wise precepts and by his noble example. Have you heard what he said of education the other day?
Cynthia.	What did he say, Dorothy?
Dorothy.	He said, "Let education, then, inspire, teach children this great truth: that God has so constituted this world into which He has sent them, that whatever is really and truly valuable may be possessed by all and possessed in exhaustless abundance."
Mrs. Peirce.	Surely, no man understands the aspirations of the human heart better than he.
Guest.	You know that it is hard for us in Nantucket to realize the great need for Normal Schools.
Another Guest.	Yes, but we owe that to the influence of Cyrus Peirce. A prophet may be without honor in his own country but happily that is not true here. I doubt if Horace Mann is any greater than Cyrus.
Mrs. Peirce.	Hush, child, how you do talk. Cyrus is a great educator, but when you talk to Horace Mann, you feel that he is imbued by some inner force that will not be denied. But here they come now.

[Cyrus Peirce, Horace Mann, *and the* Honorable Barker Burnell *enter.*]

Mrs. Peirce.	Welcome to Nantucket, Mr. Mann. You are no stranger here, Barker, but we are always glad to greet you. Cyrus, I know you've been successful. I know it by your countenance.

[*The guests are introduced.*]

MANN.   May I congratulate you on the sympathetic co-operation which you have rendered a great cause? You should be very proud of your husband, Madam. The name of Nantucket will have historical significance in this great crusade for adequate Normal Schools.

CYNTHIA.   What happened at the meeting tonight? I am just dying to know.

MANN.   The resolutions presented by your distinguished citizen, our host, were passed. It is the first great step toward our goal.

DOROTHY.   Won't you read the resolutions to us? You know we women cannot attend your meetings but we are very anxious to further the cause.

CYRUS.   [*Adjusts his glasses and reads*] "That without questioning the character of the highly respectable and useful men engaged in education, we believe that there is a lamentable deficiency of well qualified teachers, and that this deficiency is not likely to be supplied without the establishment of Normal Schools, to teach teachers how to teach.

"That a petition be presented from the town to the General Court, that our representative be instructed to urge the same on the consideration of the Legislature."

[*Guests express approval*]

MRS. PEIRCE.   We are all very happy, but here is coffee. Let us have some diversion. Cynthia will sing for us.

[*The guests stand at ease, and* CYNTHIA *sings some of the old English ballads. At the close of the singing, the guests take their leave and the lights dim down slowly.*]

SCENE 3.

The Home of Cyrus Peirce.

[*It is the twentieth of April, 1838.*]

MANN.   I tell you, Cyrus, yesterday will be a great day in the history of education. While the bells were pealing out a tribute to those heroes who fired "The shot that was heard around the world" and made the green at Lexington a hallowed spot, Governor Everett signed the order for the establishment of the first Normal School in Lexington. Our cause is won and you must be the man to direct this great experiment.

CYRUS.	I have a duty here, Horace. This is our home. It is not easy to sever old ties.
MANN.	But, Cyrus, there is no other who has caught the vision as you have done. This is a great venture which must be led by a man of training with high ideals and a sympathetic heart.
CYRUS.	I have dreamed a dream and I will dedicate myself to making that dream a reality.
MANN.	You will indeed find favor in the sight of God and of your fellow men "for all those who are worthily laboring to elevate mankind, to promote the cause of education, are laboring to elevate mankind into the upper and purer regions of civilization, Christianity, and the worship of the true God."

TABLEAU BACK

EDUCATION *is handing a certificate for teaching to* A GROUP OF TEACHERS.

SCENE 4.

[*On the back is a cut-out of the first Normal School Building at Bridgewater. Time: 1846.* HORACE MANN *is addressing a group of students.*]

MANN.	You are the only human beings whom I envy. Into your hands are put "the gay, guileless, thoughtless young". It is of these precious immortal beings that we say again "Here is a new race. Begin again." I believe Normal Schools to be a new instrumentality in the advancement of the race.
CHORUS.	Another stanza of *Land of Hope and Glory*.

FINAL TABLEAU

[*Through the gates pass a processional of teachers. The procession ends. Once more he sees a vision.* DEMOCRACY *and* EDUCATION *hold out to* THE GREAT CRUSADER *a wreath of laurel. He lays the shield of Truth at their feet and kneeling he holds forth to* DEMOCRACY *the sword of Faith.*]

EPISODE III
The Recall to the Cause of Education

CHARACTERS

EDUCATION
HORACE MANN
A YOUNG MAN
A YOUNG WOMAN
DEMOCRACY
CHORUS

SCENE I.

Cut-out of Antioch College.

[EDUCATION *brings the shield of Truth once again and the sword of Faith.*]

EDUCATION.   Once again I summon thee. You who have had the faith to make your visions realities must again gird your armor on and go forth to further the cause of education. The sons and daughters of the west need your vision and your inspiration. Again a virgin land lies fallow. Only the seed needs to be sown and the harvest will be beyond estimation. Antioch College seeks you.

MANN.   It is time to put my armor on. A new quest will be mine in this endeavor. The time has come for the establishment of equal education for both women and men. This college I will dedicate to "The Honor of God and the Service of Man." Here we will develop a new race: a body grown from its elemental beginning in health; a mind as strong for the immortal as is the body for the mortal life, and then a moral nature presiding like a divinity over the whole.

TABLEAU

EDUCATION *stands on the stairs. Just below,* HORACE MANN *is presenting a diploma to a young woman and to a young man in cap and gown.*

MANN.   Be ashamed to die until you have won some victory for humanity.

[*The lights die down.*]

CHORUS.   A verse of *"Nearer My God to Thee."*

DEMOCRACY.   A great son has laid his armor down. Bear them gently and with reverence place them in honor in the Temple of Learning. It will ever be a monument to a great crusader. A man might as well hope to dwell near the sun unmoved as not to glow when brought to feel his fervid love of truth and heart-felt zeal in its quest.

FINALE
TABLEAU AND PROCESSIONAL

DEMOCRACY *takes center place with the symbolic figures of* TRUTH *and* FAITH *on either side.* EDUCATION *holds out a laurel wreath above the head of* A KNIGHT *who represents the Great Crusader.*

A lovely processional passes, made up of several groups. [*The music for this processional could be* THE PILGRIM'S CHORUS *from Tannhauser.*]

Group 1:   Symbolic figures representing the Normal Schools: Adams, Bridgewater, Fitchburg, Framingham, Hyannis, Lowell, Salem, Westfield, Worcester.

[*This group marches around stage and then separates and stands on either side of Tableau Group.*]

Group 2:   Seekers of the Truth:
The Ancient, represented by the Magi.
The Greeks, representing Greek Culture.
The Romans, representing Law.

Group 3:   The Sciences:
Mathematics: represented by Pythagoras, Euclid, and others.
Physics: Aristotle, Archimedes, Roger Bacon, Newton, and Franklin.
Astronomy: Ptolemy, Copernicus, Galileo.
Chemistry: Robert Boyle, Sir Humphry Davy, Joseph Priestly, John Dalton, P. Curie, Mme. Curie.
Natural Sciences: Geology, Botany, and Zoology.

Group 4:   The Arts:
Sculpture, Painting
Music
Literature: English (others)
Languages: German, French, Spanish.

Group 5:   Education:
Scholars: from the early times to the present.

[*Groups 2, 3, 4, and 5 follow in procession, and then group in final Tableau.*]

CHORUS.   All sing one verse of *"America The Beautiful"*, as follows:
O beautiful for spacious skies,
For amber waves of grain,
For purple mountain majesties
Above the fruited plain!
America! America!
God shed His grace on thee,
And crown thy good with brotherhood
From sea to shining sea!

CURTAIN

"Let the next generation, then, be my client."

UNITS OF WORK

In the study of Horace Mann, and of the life, times, and social conditions in the United States in which he lived and worked, Units of Work may be arranged and carried out along modern procedure of teaching and learning.

Appropriate Units of Work will include experiences and activities in the many school subjects as well as providing opportunities for expressing the originality, initiative, and special talents of pupils.

The following problems are suggestive:

1. Horace Mann, The Children's Friend.
    (A fifth grade unit of work)
    "The Children of Massachusetts are present in my mind every day. They live in my heart. I desire to give them the blessing of deeds and sacrifices."
2. An Imaginary Visit to a Southern Planter's Home in 1837.
    (A unit for grade six)
3. Who's Who in the United States in 1837.
    (A Junior High School unit)
4. Compare the Panic of 1837 with the Present Depression.
    (A Senior High School unit)
5. The Growth and Development of the Normal Schools in Massachusetts.
    (A Teachers College project)

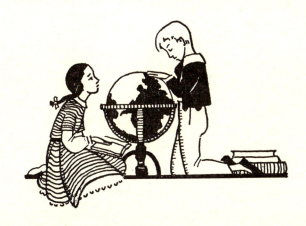

TOPICS FOR SPECIAL REPORTS OR INDIVIDUAL PROJECTS

I. 1796   Birth and Boyhood
  - A. Heredity
    1. Physical and Mental Makeup of Parents
    2. Previous Progenitors
  - B. Environment
    1. Lack of Educational Opportunities
    2. Religious Influence

II. 1816–19 Brown University (student)
  - A. Preparation For
  - B. Entrance
  - C. Career At
  - D. Graduation From
  - E. Tutor in Latin and Greek — After a Short Absence

III. 1819   Entered Office of J. J. Fiske of Wrentham to Study Law

IV. 1819   Recalled to Brown University to Tutor in Greek and Latin

V. 1821–23 Law Student at Litchfield

VI. 1823   Admitted to Norfolk County Bar
  - A. Preparation For
  - B. Passing the Bar
  - C. A Lawyer
    1. In Dedham
    2. In Boston
    3. Professional Principles
    4. Notable Orations
       - a. Fourth of July Oration that won Adams' Interest
       - b. Eulogy on Adams and Jefferson

VII. 1824   Fourth of July Oration at Dedham

VIII. 1826   Eulogy on Adams and Jefferson

IX. 1827   State Representative
  - A. Massachusetts House of Representatives
    1. Bills Sponsored

  X. 1833 State Senator
  XI. 1835 President of Senate
         A. State Senate
           1. Bills Sponsored
           2. President of the Senate
           3. Act of 1837
  XII. 1837 Secretary of Board of Education
         A. Educational Conditions Prevailing
         B. Annual Report (Stressing Seventh)
         C. Common School Journal
  XIII. 1839 Established Minimum School Year of Six Months
  XIV. 1843 Seventh Annual Report
  XV. 1848 U. S. Congress
         A. Mann, A National Figure
           1. U. S. House of Representatives
           2. Running for Governor of Massachusetts
             a. Failure
           3. Retirement from Public Life
  XVI. 1850 Controversy with Webster
  XVII. 1853 Antioch College
         A. Contributions to Education
           1. Organizational
             a. Conventions
             b. Teachers' Institutes
             c. Normal Schools
           2. Theoretic
             a. Inductive Method
             b. Abolition of Capital Punishment
             c. Parental Attitude
             d. Phonetic Method in Teaching Reading
 XVIII. 1859 Death.

COMPOSITION WORK

The following subjects are offered as appropriate for compositions by pupils of the Junior and Senior High Schools and Teachers Colleges.

The compositions may be of one paragraph in length or much longer.

1. A Brief Life of Horace Mann
2. Some Outstanding Traits of Character of Horace Mann
3. Horace Mann, the Founder of the Common Schools
4. Horace Mann, Champion of Prohibition, Public Education, and Anti-Slavery
5. The Importance of the Common Schools in American Democracy and Horace Mann's Part in their Development
6. His Alma Mater, Brown University
7. His Ideals in Work and Public Service
8. The State House in Horace Mann's Day
9. Horace Mann's Attitude Toward Public Questions
10. Horace Mann's Love for Mankind Expressed in Many Ways
11. As President of Antioch College
12. Massachusetts Normal Schools
13. The Panic of 1837

ART WORK

INTRODUCTION

Pupils may prepare original drawings, posters, or friezes appropriate for display purposes during the celebration period.

After reviewing possibilities in material and the methods of using it, it seems that a dramatization of various acts in the life of Horace Mann furnishes the best basis for art work.

Under this method, the teacher or art instructor will develop the various interests connected with the phase selected, the students will dramatize the action, to be followed by a rendering in material selected for that level.

The following outline is submitted as a guide.

GENERAL TYPES OF ACTIVITY

I. Art Appreciation Lessons (To be developed through lantern talks, picture study, museum visits, reading, etc.)
  A. Art in the World of Horace Mann —
    1. Study of architecture of the period
    2. Study of homes and public buildings. Pictures in the homes at that time.
    3. Study of furniture and household equipment.
    4. Study of costumes.
    5. Study of designs and motifs used.
    6. Study of transportation.
    7. Making of class room museum.
    8. Who were the producing artists then.
    9. Study the illustrations, the printing art, and textile design of that period.

II. Design and Lettering.
  A. Discussion and Study Topics —
    1. Design covers for written material based on Horace Mann study.
      a. Composition
      b. History
      c. Spelling
    2. Design costumes for Horace Mann dramatic productions.
    3. Design backgrounds for table projects or stage sets.
    4. Purely creative designs based on motifs used at this time. Apply.
    5. Lettering of Horace Mann quotations.
    6. Designing and lettering of posters, which might have helped in the campaigns of Horace Mann.

III. Representation and Illustration.
  A. Figure Drawing. Composition.
    1. Illustrating life and activities of Horace Mann. Suggestion — Visiting common schools.
                     — Visiting homes, etc.
      a. Develop into frieze.
    2. Posed drawing.
    3. Group drawings of figures.
           (Note — settings may be included.)
  B. Perspective Drawing. (Curvilinear, parallel and angular.)

    1. Still life.
       a. Drawing of objects used at that time.
       b. Drawing of Buildings.
       Suggestions — Old State House.
                — Customs House.
                — Old one-room school buildings, exteriors and interiors.
    2. Outdoor sketching of late colonial buildings, etc.
  C. Painting lessons. New England landscape.
    1. Mann was a lover of nature.
  D. Contrasts — Then and Now — as bases of illustrations.
  E. Story of transportation. Vehicles, etc.

IV. Construction. Structural Design.
  A. Making of booklets.
  B. Making of objects for sand table projects.
  C. Making of stage settings.
  D. Making of costumes.
  E. Making of stage properties.

V. Child Experience Programs.
  A. Making of old school house, corner of home, etc., when children can relive and play experiences.
  B. Tableaux depicting outstanding historical events and educational contributions.
  C. Pageants.
    1. Creative writing.
    2. Costumes.
    3. Settings.
    4. Sketches.
  D. Plays.
    1. Creative writing.
    2. Costumes.
    3. Drawing, painting and construction of scenery.
    4. Properties — lighting, etc.
    5. Designing programs, posters, etc.

SUGGESTED OUTLINES BY GRADES

I. Grades I, II, and III.
Early life and what he did as a boy.
Life in Franklin, Massachusetts.
The village school. The Franklin Library. Work braiding straw for hat factory.

Making of old school house, corner of home, etc., when children can relive and play experiences.

His clothes, the farm, amusements, and home.

II.   Grades IV, V, and VI.

Use of maps at this level. Trace Mann's travels in his early education, his work in Dedham, his moving to Boston, etc.

Study transportation as well, including both the forms of transportation in use in Massachusetts, in ocean travel, and in Europe.

III. Grades VII, VIII, and IX.

A study of the short quotations of Horace Mann.

Lettering of Horace Mann sayings.

Designing and lettering of posters for present day education and possibly old time education.

In connection with lettering program, these quotations should be lettered in usual small size.

Lettering should also be done on large paper or on blackboards; particularly good will be his letter of acceptance of the first Chairmanship, and excerpts from his letter of resignation.

IV.   Grades X, XI, and XII.

On this level, big poster-like drawings using figures should mainly be done.

Figure drawing — adult.

Illustrating life and activities of Horace Mann.

Suggestions — Visiting common schools.

                   — Visiting homes, etc.

a.   Develop into a frieze.

Posed drawing. (Note — have children pose in costume.)

Group drawing of figures.

Note: Settings may be included.

No portraits — represent Horace Mann as in the scene.

Trouble in Boston Schools — disagreements with the Boston School Masters.

Travel about the State — the institution of Teachers Colleges and Teachers' Conventions.

Travel in Europe — European conveyances — costumes. Observation of educational systems.

Early struggles in founding Antioch College, and education under near-wilderness conditions.

DETAILED OUTLINES BY GRADES
Grades I, II, and III.

I.   Discussion and Study Topic.
    Farm life when Horace Mann was a boy.

II. Art Subject.
    Representation.

III. Expression.
    Illustrations.

IV. Suggested topics.

  A. Home life.

    What did Horace Mann do to help about the home?
      Perhaps he brought in wood. Perhaps he fed the
      animals.

    What did he do for fun?
      He may have gone fishing. He probably knew how
      to skate.

Note: Dramatize each activity before trying to draw.
    Make a picture of a little boy helping or having fun.

Note: Children are not to be led to think of their drawings as
      pictures of little boys who lived in those early days.
    Use crayons or water colors and make large drawings.

  B. School life.

    The school was a small building — it looked a little
    like (name a local building with which the children
    are familiar). Show a picture, or better still, a
    model made of wood, cardboard or clay.

      Horace Mann walked to school carrying his book.
      What do you suppose he used to write with and
        what did he write on?
      How did the drinking water get into the school
        room?
      Make large drawings to show some of the things
      Horace Mann did in his school.

  C. Horace Mann lived in the country and loved it. He
    watched the clouds in the sky. He knew the trees
    that gave shade in the summer. He knew the trees
    that were green in the summer and yellow-red and
    orange in the autumn.

      What were some of the trees he knew so well?
      What were some of the flowers he knew?
      Try to answer these questions with large colorful
      drawings.

DETAILED OUTLINES BY GRADES
Grades IV, V, and VI.

I. Discussion and Study Topic.
>Transportation.

II. Art Subject.
>Representation.

III. Expression.
>Illustration and maps.

IV. Suggested topics.

A. Travel — trace on map the route from Franklin to Boston as it was in Horace Mann's youth — trace the route used today.

Make a drawing of one thing you will see on the road today that Horace Mann never saw or heard of.

How would Horace Mann have travelled from Franklin to Boston — by foot, by horse, by coach, by train?

Answer the question by making a drawing.

Make another drawing showing how you would travel today.

B. Horace Mann went to Europe in?

Make sketches of the type of ship in which he travelled.

Note: An illustrator often has to make his illustrations from the word descriptions that are given. Try that way of working, before you hunt for a picture. If you use a picture, be sure it is a truthful representation. Do not copy it. Study it, for its general proportions, construction and shape. Learn as much as possible from it. Then put it away and make the drawing.

Make sketches of the types of ships he might travel on today.

C. General topic — Architecture.

Discuss House Types — those of today and the yesterday which Horace Mann knew.

Make sketches of:

1. The type of gabled roof house he lived in as a boy.
2. The type he knew well in Litchfield, Conn.
3. The type of church with which he was familiar.
4. The type of public building such as the State House in Boston with its dome and its Bulfinch front.

D. Note the necessity for research — and study — use pictures only for the information they give — never copy them. Students should pose for each other when study of action is needed.

E. Completed problems may take the form of murals, posters, or illustrations.

DETAILED OUTLINES BY GRADES
Grades VII, VIII, and IX.

I. Discussion Topic.
    The sayings of Horace Mann.

II. Art Subject.
    Design.

III. Expression.
    Lettering.

IV. Suggested Topics:
    Choose a saying that suits the occasion and the age.
    Discuss the style of letter suitable.
    Consider the space to be used.
    Decide upon the medium.
    Completed problem might be:
      A. Quotation lettered at beginning of a page.
      B. On cover of booklet.
      C. On the blackboard.
      D. On a program.
      E. On a poster.
    Suggested Quotations:
    His letter of acceptance.
    From his letter of resignation.
    Quotations appropriate to present day.
    Those more specifically applicable to earlier times.

DETAILED OUTLINES BY GRADES
Grades X, XI, and XII.

I. Discussion and Study Topics.
    A. Costume of the period.
    B. Travels of Horace Mann.
    C. Dramatic incidents.
    D. Activities.
    E. Reformations.

II. Art Subject.
    A. Representation.
    B. Design.

III.　Expression.
　　　Illustration — posters — murals — illustrated decorative maps.
IV.　Suggested Topics:
　　A.　The Church Steeple that became a library.
Note:　Benjamin Franklin when asked to give money for the creation of a steeple on the church at Franklin refused, but gave a sum which must be used for books, thus starting one of the first libraries in the state.
　　B.　Making the great decision.
　　　Horace Mann makes decision — to give up law practice and serve education.
　　C.　He edits the COMMON SCHOOL.
　　　It is read in many homes.　It arouses controversial discussion.
　　D.　Horace Mann becomes a janitor.
Note:　On arriving at the place where he was to lecture he finds no preparation and the room in disorder.　He takes to the broom.
　　E.　Corporal punishments in early Boston schools.
　　　Before the protest by Mann.　After the protest by Mann.
　　F.　The first Normal School.
　　G.　Ohio and its neighbors in 1848.
Order of procedure:
　　1.　Discuss the topic.
　　2.　Make individual sketches of the idea.

The old-time schoolhouse, at Dedham, Massachusetts

"Still sits the schoolhouse by the road,
    A ragged beggar sunning;
Around it still the sumachs grow
    And blackberry vines are running."

By Whittier.

RADIO PROGRAMS

1. HORACE MANN, THE GREAT EDUCATOR
   (A Fifteen Minute Radio Broadcast — For use in
   Broadcasting Stations, or as an Imaginary Broadcast
   at Assembly in Elementary or Junior High Schools)

2. HORACE MANN AT ANTIOCH COLLEGE
   (A Radio Script — for Presentation in a Commercial
   Broadcasting Station, or at Assembly in Junior or
   Senior High Schools or Teachers Colleges)

HORACE MANN,
THE GREAT EDUCATOR

HORACE MANN, THE GREAT EDUCATOR

The name of Horace Mann . . .

HORACE MANN, THE GREAT EDUCATOR

CHARACTERS

ANNOUNCER
MISS HOLDEN *A Teacher in Modern School*
BARBARA ⎫
ARNOLD ⎬ *Pupils in Modern School*
ROGER ⎭
MRS. THOMAS MANN, *Horace's Mother*
HORACE MANN
SAMUEL JOHN BARRETT, *Horace's Teacher*
JOSIAH QUINCY ⎫
CHARLES SUMNER ⎬ *Horace Mann's Friends.*
JOHN G. WHITTIER ⎪
REV. THEODORE PARKER ⎭

ANNOUNCER. The name of Horace Mann has been acclaimed in every state in the Union. It has also been recognized in the educational life of many foreign countries. Horace Mann is entitled to be regarded as an inspired prophet of educational reform. Like Lincoln, he rose out of the very humble conditions in which he was born to great heights of achievement largely through personal consecration and conscientious effort. Let us hear what a class of older children have to say about him. The scene is the Horace Mann School in Boston, Massachusetts; the teacher, Miss Holden, is speaking. Listen.

MISS HOLDEN. Now, children, I have a pleasant surprise for you. We're going to suspend the regular order of lessons and have a questionnaire. I see you're all interested by the way you straighten up. Yes, Barbara, what is it?

BARBARA. I should like to suggest that *you* act as chairman of the forum, Miss Holden.

HOLDEN. [*Laughs*] That's very nice of you, I'm sure. All those in favor will please say "Aye".

ALL. Aye.

HOLDEN. Now, then, what subject shall we discuss? Yes, Arnold?

ARNOLD. I'd like to ask a question. This is called the Horace Mann School. Why couldn't it be named after some great athelete like Babe Ruth?

HOLDEN.	Would you say Babe Ruth was a great athelete, Arnold?
ARNOLD.	No, Miss Holden, he was a great ball-player, the Home Run King.
HOLDEN.	True, that made him a great athlete, not athelete. Now for Your question: This school was named years before Babe Ruth was born. Does anyone know who Horace Mann was?
ALL.	He was a great teacher.
HOLDEN.	Splendid! And isn't it more logical to name a school after a teacher than after even so great a ball-player as Babe Ruth, Roger?
ROGER.	It's awful hard to hit as many homeruns as Babe Ruth did.
HOLDEN.	Yes, I suppose it is. But isn't it also hard to plan for a whole educational system as Horace Mann did? How many of you would like to see the name of this school changed? [*Pause*] About half. How many of you know a great deal about Babe Ruth? [*Pause*] I see; practically all of you. And how many know something about Horace Mann? [*Pause*] Only two or three. Then suppose we see what we can find out. Barbara, will you start the ball rolling?
BARBARA.	I think Horace Mann was born on Feb. 22, 1795.
HOLDEN.	Yes, Roger, what is it?
ROGER.	I looked in the encyclopedia, and his birthday was May 4, 1796.
HOLDEN.	That is correct. Dates are not the most important, but if we use them, we must be sure that they are right. You may go on, Roger. Where was he born?
ROGER.	In Franklin, Massachusetts. His Father was Thomas Mann, and they were very poor.
HOLDEN.	And how did that affect his chance for an education, Arnold?
ARNOLD.	He couldn't get any. His father and mother believed in education, but they couldn't afford it.
HOLDEN.	Very good. When Horace was thirteen, his father died. Up to the age of fifteen, he had never been to school more than eight to ten weeks in any one year. But the home atmosphere was such as to give him a strong desire for learning. His mother was talking it over with young Horace one day . . .
[*Fading out*] [*Fading in*]	
MRS. MANN.	Aye, my son, a good education is a grand thing. And it was thy father's wish that the opportunity might be given thee.
HORACE.	I know. I do not blame you for my misfortune. If I rebel at all, it is against the hard conditions which oppress us. To be "nursed in toil" may be a good idea, but you can

have too much even of a good thing. Education ought to be made easier to get.

MRS. MANN. Never mind, my son, I know thou'rt not happy. But be of good cheer. Dost thou know what I have planned for thee?

HORACE. How can I until you tell me?

MRS. MANN. Well, I have arranged to have Mr. Barrett come here and teach thee.

HORACE. You don't mean Samuel John Barrett, the great teacher?

MRS. MANN. Mr. Barrett is coming here to give thee lessons for six months.

HORACE. How wonderful! I can scarcely believe it.

MRS. MANN. But there is one condition: thou must not neglect thy work.

HORACE. Oh, I won't, mother, believe me. I'll gladly work my fingers to the bone if I can only get the opportunity to learn something and be somebody.

MRS. MANN. Very well. Mr. Barrett writes me that he will be here
[*Fading out*] tomorrow morning to begin thy instruction . . .
[*Fading in*]

BARRETT. [*Pompously*] I understand you have had few advantages, Horace.

HORACE. But my parents have done all they could.

BARRETT. No parent has done all he can unless he has furnished his
 * children with a good classical education.

HORACE. But, Sir, that was beyond their means, and my mother is a widow. And I am young, Mr. Barrett, I can learn.

BARRETT. Yes, yes, of course. I do not mean to imply that your people are not estimable. Quite the contrary. They are the salt of the earth; none better, my boy. But a tree is known by its fruits. Now, you —

HORACE. Pardon me, Sir. if I am not a credit to my mother, it is not for lack of trying. Believe me, I *am* ambitious to learn and to succeed.

BARRETT. Have you any books?

HORACE. Yes, Sir, here they are.

BARRETT. Hm-m. You take pretty good care of them, don't you?

HORACE. They were my father's books, sir. I have never abused a book in my life.

BARRETT. There are no pencil marks here and no corners turned down that I can see.

HORACE. Mr. Barrett, I would as soon think of sticking a pin in my own flesh as to mistreat a book. To me they are just like living creatures.

BARRETT. Well said, my lad. Have you had much formal schooling?

HORACE.	Not more than 8 or 10 weeks a year, Sir.
BARRETT.	Hm-m. I shall have to give you a test. It will be difficult to prepare you for college in six months. Do you think you can do it?
HORACE.	[*Eagerly*] O, yes, Sir, with your help I can do anything.
BARRETT.	You flatter me, my boy, but I admire your spirit, and, as Cicero says, it is the spirit that counts. I have here a copy of his "Select Orations", which I shall loan you now that I know it will be in good hands. Where is your Bible?
HORACE.	It is here, Sir.
BARRETT.	How about the New Testament, how many gospels are there?
HORACE.	Four: Matthew, Mark, Luke, and John.
BARRETT. [*Fading out*]	That is right. And they all deal with the life and work of our Lord and Master. The first three deal mainly with —
HOLDEN.	And so in six months Horace Mann prepared for the sophomore class at Brown University. It was hard work and meant many hours spent in serious study when the boy might well have longed to join the other boys in their simple but joyful sports. At college he went at his studies as though he intended to finish in one year. That was the way he tackled everything. Later in life, when he was called to the Secretaryship of the Massachusetts Board of Education, he showed the same singleness of purpose. He gave up his law practice and resigned from the Legislature, where he had served with distinction. He gave himself whole-heartedly to the great educational work, but he made a close study of education in all its branches before he went to work. One of his favorite ideas was training schools for teachers. Here we find him bursting into the office of his friend, Josiah Quincy. Listen: [*Sound. Door Opens*]
HORACE.	Mr. Quincy! Mr. Quincy! [*Sound. Door closes*]
QUINCY.	Yes, Horace, what is it?
HORACE.	Mr. Quincy, would you like to go to Heaven?
QUINCY	Why — yes — but not immediately. Why?
HORACE.	But eventually. Then I have arranged for your admission.
QUINCY.	Will you please stop talking in riddles and tell me what this is all about?
HORACE.	Excuse me, in the excitement I forgot. You know we have to move the Normal School from Lexington.
QUINCY.	Yes, I understand your idea has grown so that the building there is too small.

HORACE.	Exactly. Now I have found a new location at Fuller's Academy in West Newton, which is a very desirable location, but unfortunately, the funds of the Board are too low to buy it —
QUINCY.	So you want me to advance the money, is that it? How much do you need?
HORACE.	Only $1,500. Of course, when the school is through with the property, title can revert to you.
QUINCY.	$1,500. All right, here is your check, Horace.
HORACE.	Thank you, Mr. Quincy. You have just bought yourself the highest seat in the Kingdom of Heaven.
QUINCY.	[*Laughs*] And a mighty good bargain, too. [*Pause*] Before you go, Horace, I might as well tell you that I don't want that property back. When I give anything —
HORACE.	Very well, then, title can revert to the state.
QUINCY. [*Fading out*]	You are too unselfish. I shall see to it that ownership of the property is transferred to you when the Normal School is through with it —
HOLDEN.	Horace Mann had a frank and open nature. He also expressed himself with vigor and conviction. So it was natural that he should make enemies. Some of his Annual Reports, while well written and in the main truthful, aroused the opposition of some of the teachers in the Boston Public Schools. The masters were also educated men and they resented Horace Mann's criticism of them and their methods. A long controversy developed, but in the end Horace Mann was vindicated. Here we have some of his friends gathered in the office of Josiah Quincy. In the group besides Quincy are Charles Sumner, Edward Everett, John G. Whittier, Henry Wilson, Anson P. Burlingame, Rev. Theodore Parker, and a number of business and professional men. Mr. Quincy is speaking:
QUINCY.	Gentlemen: I have taken the liberty of calling you together for the purpose of finding some means to aid our friend, Horace Mann, in his work as Secretary of the Board of Education. Mr. Sumner, you know something about his condition.
SUMNER.	Yes. I have here a note that he wrote to his physician. [*Reads*] "Can you do anything for a brain that has not slept for three weeks? I can feel a flame in the center of my cranium, blazing and flaring around like a pile of brush burning in the wind. What can you do to extinguish it?" He is in a bad way, do you not think so, Mr. Whittier?

WHITTIER.	I think he has been working too hard. Why could we not band ourselves together to support him in his work? I am sure that his ideas are sound and his motives are above reproach.
QUINCY.	That is what I have felt from the beginning. It is true that he is impulsive and sometimes exaggerates the case which he is presenting, but he is honest and sincere and does not venture an opinion unless he has taken the trouble to post himself on the subject. I should like to have an expression from the Rev. Theodore Parker.
PARKER.	I am most heartily in favor of Mr. Mann and his progressive ideas. I think we ought to organize ourselves into a voluntary committee to back him up and also to raise a fund for the purpose of carrying his ideas into effect.

[*Fading out*]
[*Fading in*]

| MANN. | Investigation shows that there is one pitfall into which the young of our day are in danger of falling. Men are rapidly coming to the worship of wealth. But what is the accumulation of wealth to the labors of a Benjamin Franklin, a George Washington, or a Dr. Bowditch? It is true we all have a duty to accumulate for a rainy day, but in the duty of accumulation, all above a fortune is a misfortune. The day is sure to come when man will look back upon the rule of Money with as severe and as just a condemnation as we now look back upon the predatory chieftains of the Dark Ages. |

[All: Applause]

MANN.	But Mr. Chairman and gentlemen, you must pardon this digression from the subject in hand. As I understand it, you have come together as friends of the Massachusetts Board of Education.
QUINCY.	We have, Mr. Mann, and we have come to certain definite conclusions. Mr. Parker, will you please read our recommendations?
PARKER.	With pleasure. First of all, we have passed a unanimous vote of confidence in the Board of Education and in you, Mr. Mann, as its Secretary. Next, we intend to interest ourselves in the election of proper school boards, the inspection of grammar schools, and the selection of efficient teachers and masters. We have also pledged ourselves to raise $5,000 for the purpose of improving the normal schools of the state.

QUINCY. And that is not all, Mr. Mann. What about the Legislature, Mr. Sumner?

SUMNER. We propose to ask the Legislature for another $5,000. That will give the Board of Education a total of $10,000 for the normal schools.

[All: Applause]

MANN. The expressions of your sympathy and practical support in this crucial hour almost unman me. The subject of popular education has had my intensive interest for several years. If I have erred, it has been on the side of too great an interest and intensity. Among other things, I have commended science as an improver of the mind. A knowledge of chemistry will make the notion of charms and philters ridiculous; a knowledge of nature will banish fairies and ghosts and witches from all respectable society; the science of astronomy will sweep all the terrors and follies of astrology from the heavens. If men can love fiction, they can love science better. No invention of the imagination is so exciting as the revelations of science. Amid the wonders which science is yet to unfold, the wonders of Aladdin's lamp will lose their splendor. Education gives the young man opportunities where, day by day, he may build himself up into the likeness of the great universe in which he dwells, imitating its strength as well as its beauty, and aspiring to its moral heights as well as expanding his knowledge of its physical amplitude.

[Fading out]
HOLDEN. And that, in brief, is the story of Horace Mann. He lived to be 63 years of age and his life was devoted to great and noble causes. How many of you know more about him now than you did a while ago? *[Pause]* And will all those who are in favor of keeping the name "Horace Mann School," please say "Aye"?

ALL. Aye! Aye!

HOLDEN. Very well. You are dismissed.

FINIS

The modern "Horace Mann School", Franklin, Massachusetts

HORACE MANN
AT ANTIOCH COLLEGE

HORACE MANN AT ANTIOCH COLLEGE

In September, 1853 . . .

HORACE MANN AT ANTIOCH COLLEGE

CHARACTERS

NARRATOR
MRS. MANN
SWETT
MR. MANN
CHILD
CLARA
SUE
TOM
STEWARDESS
MR. SNOW
MR. SHAW

NARRATOR. In September, 1853, Horace Mann left Massachusetts to accept the position as President of Antioch College in Ohio. Mann succeeded in carrying out on a higher plane and in a more mature way the same ideals which he had held in the matter of public schools. With such modification as was necessary, he applied these ideals in college administration. Mr. Mann's reputation for scholarship gave him much influence. As a result, what were then considered radical educational ideas were received from him with respect. This distinguished man faced many problems in the early days of Antioch. Yet the students rejoiced in the leadership of a man so earnest, so devoted, and so noble. The slow train on which he is riding is drawing up to a small railroad station in Ohio. Listen!

[*Sound of train and whistle drawing closer to microphone, and stopping.*]

MRS. MANN. So this is Yellow Springs!

SWETT. Mr. Mann?

MANN. Yes, I am Mr. Mann.

SWETT. How do you do, Sir? My name is Swett, member of the Antioch College Committee.

MANN. Yes, yes, — er —

SWETT. I'm sorry, but I was the only member of the Committee able to meet you.

MANN. That's quite all right. I understand the circumstances. My dear, this is Mr. Swett. Mr. Swett, my wife.

MRS. MANN.   How do you do?

SWETT.   Delighted to meet you, Mrs. Mann. And these boys are your children?

MRS. MANN.   Yes, our three sons.

SWETT.   Splendid. My carriage is right over here. The college is about three miles up the road and if we hurry, we can get there before the sun sets.

MANN.   Yes, of course. Boys, you carry the smaller pieces.

[*Sounds of getting into carriage.*]

SWETT.   Gid-dap, gid-dap, tch, tch. —

[*Sounds of horses' hoofs and carriage wheels continuing to specified stop.*]

MANN.   Tell me, Mr. Swett, how are things progressing? Is the college ready to open next week?

SWETT.   Well, not exactly. We've been short-handed for labor. You see, harvest time takes every available man.

MANN.   Oh. [*Slight pause*] Ah, these extensive fields!

SWETT.   Yes?

MANN.   To me they are symbolic.

MRS. MANN.   Symbolic of what, Horace?

SWETT.   They strike me as being merely a picture of desolation.

MANN.   That may be so — but to me they express freedom, freedom from all that has been imprisoned or darkened through the agency of man.

MRS. MANN.   [*Laughing gently*] My husband is in an exalted state of mind, Mr. Swett.

MANN.   But think of the opportunity that lies ahead — opportunity for great labor. My great opportunity!

SWETT.   Just what do you mean, Mr. Mann?

MANN.   I mean an opportunity to put into practice at Antioch certain educational theories that have been simmering in my mind. Coeducation, non-sectarianism.

SWETT.   That sounds mighty fine, but I reckon you've got a task on your hands. People 'round these parts are somewhat obligated.

MRS. MANN.   I tried to explain to Horace that people here would perhaps resent any contemplated upheaval of education.

MANN.   I know, I know. But future vegetation depends upon what kind of seed is sown. And just think, an opportunity for science to come into its own!

SWETT.   I understand you hope to include art and music in the curriculum?

MANN.   Yes, indeed. With the refining influences of art and music we can accomplish wonders. And I shall give such attention to health as other institutions have not yet conceived.

SWETT.   Look! There's the college now. Those brick towers are the towers of Antioch! Get along there, gid-dap, gid-dap, tch, tch.

[*Sound of horses' hoofs quickened*]

SWETT.   Whoa, whoa!

[*Sound of hoofs and wheels discontinued*]

SWETT.   Here we are. It's still light enough for you to see your way about.

MANN.   Mr. Swett, that building is only partially erected!

SWETT.   Well, I told you it wasn't quite ready.

MANN.   I know, but I hardly expected it to be in this unfinished state.

CHILD.   Dad, I'm hungry. I want to go to our house.

MRS. MANN. Yes, I think that is an excellent idea.

SWETT.   Well, to tell you the truth, ma'am, we haven't gotten around to a site for your house, let alone the building of it.

MANN.   Do you mean to say that no accommodations have been made for my family and myself?

SWETT.   That's just about it! But wait, I think we'll be able to convince Mr. Black to open his boarding house. It's closed now, the summer season being over.

MRS. MANN. But certainly the house will be in no condition for occupancy. If it's closed, that means that there is no means of heating it?

SWETT.   That's true, but I can see no other way out.

MANN.   It's a ridiculous situation. Come, my dear, somehow we shall make it habitable and somehow we shall have the college in a presentable condition for the inauguration.

MRS. MANN. It seems to me, Horace, a matter both for laughter and for tears.

MANN.   [*Laughing gently*] Yes, my dear, yet we shall come through victoriously. The standards of Antioch will be high in scholarship, teaching, and morals.

[*Music*]

NARRATOR. Despite the drawbacks of a partly finished building and inadequate accommodations, Horace Mann presented his inaugural address on the fifth of October. It is now three days later in the combination lecture-hall-dining-room.

[*Fading in*]

[*Sounds of boys and girls laughing and talking, clatter of china*]

CLARA.   Doesn't it seem funny, Sue, to have the President of the College eating at the same table as the students?

SUE.   Yes, Clara, it does. But you know, I sort of like it. He isn't like other Presidents, or teachers as far as that goes.

Tom.   At other colleges, fellows and girls can't even talk to each
                other. But Mr. Mann, he's great. He sort of makes things
                pleasant and cheerful — makes a fellow feel at ease.

Sue.   Hush, Tommy! Mr. Mann is signaling for attention.

Tom.   Say, that's great. Been here three days now and it's the
                first time.

[Sounds fading out]
[Fading in]

Mann.   It's with great pride that I glance over this more or less
                makeshift lecture–dining hall. Three days ago you were
                amongst a group of several hundred applicants. But today,
                you young men and women represent but a small percentage
                of that number. It is you who have the qualifications and
                have passed the most rigid of examinations. Be proud of
                that, as proud as I. Remember, however, that there will
                be hardships, hardships denying you many physical con-
                veniences — and yet, your studies must and will go on.
                There will be no place for the lazy. Let me add but one
                more thing. Antioch College will have no system of honors
                or prizes. There will be no appealing motives where the
                triumph of one involves the defeat of another. It is un-
                christian to place you young folks in a position where for
                one to succeed is for another to fail. I appeal to your
                hunger for knowledge and ask you to be better in every
                department of life tomorrow than you have been today.

[Sounds of applause]

Narrator.   It did not take Mann very long to realize that he would meet
                with strong opposition. Instead of working in close har-
                mony with Mann, the Antioch College Committee took
                many steps to provide friction. This was done simply be-
                cause Mann would not, and could not, conform to their
                ideas. It is now about a year later. Mr. Snow, the super-
                intendent and the stewardess are talking:

[Fading in]

Stewardess.   Mr. Mann wants to see you, Mr. Snow.

Snow.   What's he want now?

Stewardess.   Wal', I'm certain I wouldn't be a-knowin'.

Snow.   Allus a-crabbin' about somethin'. Him and his high falutin'
                eastern airs!

Stewardess.   You better not talk so loud, the kids might hear you.

Snow.   What if they do?

Stewardess.   Wal', they like him a powerful lot and might run and tell him.

SNOW.   Hm! Wal', I'll show him who's boss 'round these parts. One word from me and the College Committee will tell him a thing or two.

[*Fading out*]

[*Slight interval of music*]

[*Fading in*]

[*Sound of knock on door*]

MANN.   [*Behind door*] Come in.

[*Sound of door opening and closing*]

SNOW.   You wanted to see me, Mr. Mann?

MANN.   Yes, I did. It's about time you and I had a talk.

SNOW.   About what?

MANN.   Mr. Snow, first let me make it clear that you are the superintendent of Antioch.

SNOW.   Wal', I knew that right along.

MANN.   You neglect, however, to bear in mind that I am the President.

SNOW.   Is that —

MANN.   Let me finish. Mr. Snow, you have taken on a great number of duties and privileges which belong strictly to the President.

SNOW.   [*Blustering*] Well, now —

MANN.   Wait. You have chosen without my consent or consultation, teachers whom I deem incompetent for this faculty.

SNOW.   The committee gave me the power to do that.

MANN.   Really? Without asking my opinion?

SNOW.   You'll have to ask them.

MANN.   I mean to. And just what are your plans for the completion of the college and its grounds?

SNOW.   When I get the money, I'll continue. But from the way things look, I don't think there'll be any money.

MANN.   But the students are walking in mud up to their ankles, and the classrooms are still inadequately heated.

SNOW.   Wal' now, that's nothing to be worried about. Youngsters 'round these parts are brought up right, used to little things like that.

MANN.   I don't intend to let this matter drop. It is unthinkable that the teachers and students should endanger their health. I am going to call a meeting of the committee.

SNOW.   Wal', you can if you want to, but I wouldn't expect too much if I were you. Good-day.

MANN.   We shall see.

[*Fading out*]

[*Sound of door opening and closing*]

NARRATOR.   Sometime later Horace Mann calls a meeting of the Antioch
             College Committee. Mr. Shaw is the spokesman for this
             group.

MANN.   I have asked you gentlemen of the Committee to meet today
             in order to clarify the situation that now confronts us.

SHAW.   Be more specific, Mr. Mann.

MANN.   I will be, Mr. Shaw.

SHAW.   First let me say this, Mr. Mann.

MANN.   Yes?

SHAW.   You know, of course, the reasons why the President of this
             committee resigned?

MANN.   Vaguely.

SHAW.   I will come to the point then. You have consistently refused
             to dismiss the two young ladies of color from this college.
             Mr. Lowell is a righteous man. He does not consider it
             in good taste to have this mixture of races. Subsequently
             he has withdrawn his daughters from the college and,
             more important, his financial aid. There are many more
             like him.

MANN.   I am extremely sorry for that. I see, however, no solution.

             [*Sound of murmurs from men*]

SHAW.   Mr. Mann, the financial status of this college is precarious.
             I think it your duty and within your power not to alienate
             those who might contribute to its support.

MANN.   To the members of this Committee, let me make myself clear.
             I will not, and cannot, refuse the applications of anybody
             if he or she is suitably prepared to enter. It is contrary
             to justice and freedom.

SHAW.   Well, then —

MANN.   And let me add, the powers you have given to Mr. Snow, the
             superintendent, are grossly ill used. He has taken it upon
             himself to make decisions that should rightly be entirely
             out of his jurisdiction. Teachers, who in his judgment, are
             not suitable, are dismissed by him. He selects those who
             in my judgment are unfit. He has in more than one in-
             stance instigated dissension among the students and the
             faculty.

SHAW.   Perhaps that is so.

MANN.   There can be no divided authority. All friction must be
             eradicated if this college is to function normally.

SHAW.   Are you aware, Mr. Mann, that there are rumors of your
             being untrue to the Christian denomination? Of being
             untrue to every standard of honesty?

MANN.   I assume that there is a reflection on my choice of teachers. That is, when looking into the qualifications of a candidate I say, has the applicant the attainments to fit him for the position, instead, as many of you wish, does he agree sufficiently with us in religious opinion?

SHAW.   These teachers have not been of the Christian denomination.

MANN.   Sir, one of the principles distinctly set forth by the founders of this college was that Antioch should be completely non-sectarian.

SHAW.   Mr. Mann, why not use a little common sense, a little tact? We are losing many supporters through your many dispositions. We are desperately trying to avoid bankruptcy.

MANN.   We cannot possibly desist.

SHAW.   Wait, please —

MANN.   Gentlemen, [*sharply*] I have a great deal of admiration and respect for the broadminded and cultivated members of the Christian denomination. I myself have recently joined the Church. But I doubt if many of you realize the full meaning of the term "non-sectarian". From the start I have faced bitter opposition. You gentlemen hold the purse strings; do you, however, know the needs of an institution of learning?

SHAW.   I see that there can be no reasoning with you.

MANN.   What is right, is right.

[*Music*]

NARRATOR.   In spite of the frantic efforts of Horace Mann and some of his loyal friends to prevent the college from going into a state of insolvency, Mr. Snow in no uncertain terms tells him about what was one of the saddest episodes of his life. It is now mid-winter in the year 1859 —

[*Fading in*]

[*Sound of door opening and closing*]

MANN.   Mr. Snow!

SNOW.   Yeah?

MANN.   Is it true?

SNOW.   Is what true?

MANN.   That Antioch is in a state of bankruptcy?

SNOW.   That's just about the size of it. Yep, the College Committee has declared the college for sale. It's to be auctioned off to the highest bidder on the 20th of April.

NARRATOR.   And so, despite Horace Mann's super efforts, on April 20, 1859, Antioch went under the hammer. Yet, it was the best thing that could have happened. About a week later, after the sale of the college to Frank Palmer for $40,200,

Horace Mann is discussing with his wife the state of affairs as they existed then.

[*Fading in*]

MANN.   Mary, I have good news.

MRS. MANN.   You have? I can only hope it's good news for you.

MANN.   It is. Frank Palmer, who bought the college, has agreed to turn it over to a closed board, consisting of such able men as Josiah Quincy and Eli Fay.

MRS. MANN.   And you?

MANN.   And I, my dear, will continue as President.

MRS. MANN.   What about the rest of the staff?

MANN.   Ah, my dear, that's just it. I now have the full power to appoint my own staff. And that is half the battle. With this more liberal board of trustees, I shall be able to continue as I hoped when I first came. Think, an opportunity to make Antioch one of the great institutions of knowledge!

NARRATOR.   In face of much bitterness from those of the staff whom he had been compelled to dismiss, Mann succeeded in overcoming much of the opposition against the college. In the six years that he inspired the educational forces of the West from Antioch College, he influenced directly and indirectly, hundreds of youths. All through the West today are leaders of thought who owe their inspiration for scholarship and for noble living to Horace Mann's principles. In a word, the college continued because Horace Mann believed in it.

The Horace Mann Statue, State House grounds,
Boston, Massachusetts

SUGGESTED PERMANENT MEMORIAL

1. A picture of Horace Mann in every school in Massachusetts.

2. Planting Horace Mann Trees.

A PICTURE OF HORACE MANN IN EVERY SCHOOL IN MASSACHUSETTS

The hanging of a picture of Horace Mann, or the unveiling of a sculptured memorial in every school building in Massachusetts could be set as one of the activities of Education Week in 1937, and would fittingly complete the year's program.

PLANTING HORACE MANN TREES

An appropriate activity would be the planting of a tree on the school grounds. These trees should be known as "Horace Mann" Trees. Exercises appropriate for the occasion might be held.

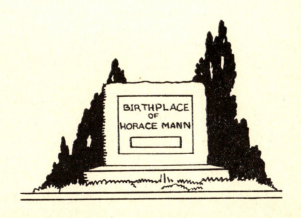

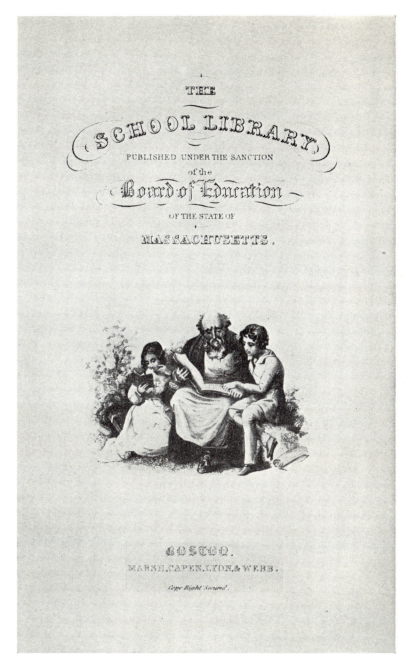

Title page of "The School Library," published under the sanction of the
Massachusetts Board of Education, January 1, 1841.
(Courtesy of Division of State Libraries)

OUTLINE OF THE LIFE OF
HORACE MANN

AN OUTLINE OF THE LIFE OF HORACE MANN

Born May 4, 1796 . . .

AN OUTLINE OF THE LIFE OF HORACE MANN

1796   Born May 4, at Franklin, Mass. One of five children of Thomas and Rebecca (Stanley) Mann. Lineal descendant of William Mann, early settler of Cambridge, Mass. Son of poor parents. Frail constitution but highly idealistic character. Hard work on farm. Braided straw on wintry nights.

1809   Early death of father magnified influence of mother. Vigorous and reactionary influence of Calvinist pastor, Rev. Nathaniel Emmons. Completely overcome after death of brother. Poor schooling and equally poor town library.

1816   Contact with eccentric but brilliant itinerant teacher, Samuel John Barrett. Intensive preparation to enter Brown University.

Successful educational pursuit, entering after six months into the sophomore class. Hard work to support self. Duty to family; tutoring.

Increased social consciousness and effect on Dr. Messer's family. Interest in daughter, Charlotte Messer, his future wife.

1819   Graduation with high honors from the University with commencement address revealing promise of Mann's faith in education as prime tool in the "accelerating improvability of the race".

Entered law office of Honorable J. J. Fiske, Wrentham, for few months. Eager acceptance of opportunity to tutor in Latin and Greek at Brown.

1821   Departure from Brown to study at Litchfield, Conn., under Judge Gould. Acknowledgment as finest student with assured success upon graduation.

1823   Admitted to the Massachusetts bar; entered law office of James Richardson in Dedham, and continued successful practice of law for a period of fourteen years.

1824   Began an active interest in public affairs.

Fourth of July oration at Dedham attracted attention of John Quincy Adams.

1826   Eulogy on Adams and Jefferson at Dedham.

1827	Beginning of interest in legislation for all phases of public welfare.
1830	Married to Charlotte Messer on September 12, 1830.
(1827–33)	House member.
1832	Death of wife August 1, 1832.
1833	Moved to Boston to continue a successful practice of law.
	Death of wife previous August a shock.
1833–37	Senate member.
1835–37	Senate President. Aided formulation of education bill with pioneer, James G. Carter. Contemporary interest in anti-alcoholic beverage usage; anti-lottery traffic; and especially the establishment of State Hospitals for the Insane.
1837	As President of Senate signed act creating State Board of Education. Accepted membership on Board of Education. Resigned to accept surprise
P	election as Secretary of Board. Recognition of intense
R	enthusiasm for educational reform as well as states-
O	manship. Acquisition of many friends who aided him
G	— despite severe attitude on moralities and general
R	prejudices. Interested in George Combe sufficiently
A	to lean backwards in adoption of his phrenology
M	philosophy.
	Two-fold campaign was arousal of public conscious-ness of need of education and the enactment of legis-lation to bring reforms into effect. Held public meetings and emphasized ideals by powerful speeches. Fiery orations kept issue alive and sustained admira-tion for the man and his cause.
	Interest in better training of teachers by a system of county conference institutes conducted by leading educators of Massachusetts and other states.
1839	Sold own law library to help erect building for first Normal School at Lexington — first of three. Active in collection of ample statistics.
	Took upon himself the tremendous task of collating all city and town school reports more thoroughly than the abstracts had heretofore been prepared.
	Under Mann's influence, a minimum school year of six months was established by an act passed in 1839.
(1838 on)	Establishment of a periodical, THE COMMON SCHOOL JOURNAL, to influence the educational public in Massachusetts. An independent publica-

tion which proved highly successful in denoting the sad condition of the state's educational level; pointing out necessary reforms; recognizing eventual progress. Of no remunerative purpose.

Publication of the twelve reports, prepared by Mann as Secretary, of the condition of education in Massachusetts and elsewhere, including a discussion of the aims, purposes, and means of education.

1843 Trip to Europe for his health and for study of European educational systems after marriage to Mary Tyler Peabody on May 1, sister of wife of Nathaniel Hawthorne. Most fruitful of his reports — the seventh — dealt with his five months' observations of educational systems in England, Ireland, Scotland, Holland, Belgium, France, and especially Germany and Switzerland.

(1844) His high commendation of German schools interpreted as critical of American institutions and a mandate for reform. The natural result was a bitter controversy from which Mann emerged even more triumphant than ever.

The companion attack on Mann was the expression of the religious sectarians against his possible establishment of "a godless system of schools". Mann's Unitarian opinion and encouragement of Bible reading without comment ran an acrimonious gauntlet.

1848 Skillful administration had brought prestige, hence his resignation of the Secretaryship to accept a seat in Congress, to which he was elected to fill the vacated place of John Quincy Adams.

1850 Deliberate sacrifice of a political career for public service.

Definite break with Daniel Webster and Whigs on compromise issue, but reelected to Congress on independent ticket.

1852 Defeated as Free-Soil candidate for governor of Massachusetts. Lack of sympathy with political life and intense interest in opportunity to try long thought-of educational reforms, influenced acceptance of presidency of Antioch College in Ohio. Had effected no national aid to education while in Congress.

1853 Settlement with wife on muddy Little Miami River for courageous new work — this time in higher education.

Personal aggressiveness still alienated faculty members and churchmen who resented his centralized authority. Yet, despite this animus and financial obligations, the ideals of Mann were realized in co-education, non-sectarianism, elective courses, anti-competitive spirit as useless emulation, character emphasis, inclusion of hygiene in curriculum, encouragement of student assumption of degree of responsibility for a government of self-discipline. Indeed a tribute to a liberal and far sighted reformer who, if he was not original, at least proved a capable synthesizer.

1859   Died August 2, 1859, at Antioch College, Yellow Springs, Ohio, with a confident vision of accomplishment and progress to come.

BIBLIOGRAPHY

BIBLIOGRAPHY

Horace Mann . . .

HORACE MANN

Bibliography

Allen, Lucy Ellis
WEST NEWTON HALF A CENTURY AGO.* 1917

Antioch Press
EDUCATION FOR DEMOCRACY; A SYMPOSIUM. 1937

Barnard, Henry
BIOGRAPHICAL SKETCH OF HORACE MANN.*
Barnard's American Journal of Education. 1858. Vol. V. pp. 609–656.

Compayré, G.
HORACE MANN ET L'ÉCOLE PUBLIQUE AUX ETAS-UNIS.*
Paris.
HORACE MANN AND THE PUBLIC SCHOOL IN THE UNITED
STATES.
Same, translated by Mary D. Frost. 1907.

Culver, R. B.
HORACE MANN AND RELIGION IN THE MASSACHUSETTS
PUBLIC SCHOOLS. 1929.

Dedham Historical Society
HORACE MANN*
Dedham Historical Register. 1895. Vol. VI. pp. 16–20.

Harris, William T.
HORACE MANN,* An address before the National Education Asso-
ciation, Buffalo, New York, July 7, 1896.
Report of United States Commissioner of Education. 1895–1896. Vol. I,
pt. I., pp. 887–897.
Bibliography, pp. 897–927. (About 700 items).

Hinsdale, B. A.
HORACE MANN AND THE COMMON SCHOOL REVIVAL IN
THE UNITED STATES. 1898. (Bibliography, pp. 311–319.)

Hubbell, George Allen
HORACE MANN, EDUCATOR, PATRIOT AND REFORMER:
A STUDY IN LEADERSHIP.* 1910.

Hubbell, George Allen
HORACE MANN IN OHIO: A STUDY OF THE APPLICATION
OF HIS PUBLIC SCHOOL IDEALS TO COLLEGE ADMINISTRA-
TION. 1900.

*Out of print.

Hubbell, George Allen
HORACE MANN AND ANTIOCH COLLEGE.*
Ohio Archaeological and Historical Society Publications. 1905. Vol. 14, pp. 12–27.

Lang, Ossian Herbert
HORACE MANN, HIS LIFE AND EDUCATIONAL WORK.* 1893.

Mann, Mary Peabody
LIFE OF HORACE MANN, by HIS WIFE.* 1865.

Martin, G. H.
EVOLUTION OF THE MASSACHUSETTS PUBLIC SCHOOL SYSTEM: A HISTORICAL SKETCH. 1915. (pp. 157–181 deal with Horace Mann.)

Mayo, Amory Dwight
HORACE MANN AND THE GREAT REVIVAL OF THE AMERICAN COMMON SCHOOLS, 1830–1850.* Report of the United States Commissioner of Education, 1896–97. Vol. I. pp. 745–767.

Phelps, W. F.
HORACE MANN, 1879.*

Sabin, Henry
HORACE MANN'S COUNTRY SCHOOL.*
Proceedings of the National Education Association. 1894. pp. 204–210.

Slosson, Edwin Emery
THE AMERICAN SPIRIT IN EDUCATION: A CHRONICLE OF GREAT TEACHERS.* 1921. (Horace Mann and the American School. pp. 124–140.)

Thurber, C. H.
HORACE MANN THE EDUCATOR STATESMAN.* May 29, 1896. University Record, Vol. I. pp. 161–165.

Wilbur, Eliza Scott (Mann)
HORACE MANN'S HOME LIFE AS SEEN BY A SPRINGFIELD WOMAN WHO SPENT PART OF HER CHILDHOOD IN THE MANN FAMILY.*
Springfield (Massachusetts) Sunday Republican, May 10, 1896.

Williams, E. I. F.
HORACE MANN: EDUCATIONAL STATESMAN. 1937.

Winship, Albert E.
GREAT AMERICAN EDUCATORS. 1900.
(Horace Mann, America's Greatest Educational Leader, pp. 15–51.)

Winship, Albert E.
HORACE MANN THE EDUCATOR.* 1896.

*Out of print.